# FRONTIERS
## THE WORLD'S GREATEST HIKES

**TRAIL**
MAGAZINE

# FRONTIERS
## The World's Greatest Hikes

MAGAZINE

Materials © Emap Active Limited 2003
Compilation and cover design © Haynes Publishing 2003

First published in 2003

A catalogue record for this book is available from the British Library

ISBN 1 84425 088 1

Published jointly by
Haynes Publishing, Sparkford,
Yeovil, Somerset BA22 7JJ, England
Phone 01963 440635,
www.haynes.co.uk
And
Emap Active Limited,
Wentworth House, Wentworth Street,
Peterborough PG1 1DS, England
Phone 01733 213700,
www.emap.com

Produced for Haynes Publishing and Emap Active Ltd by
PAGEOne, 5 Missenden Road, Chesham, Bucks HP5 1JL, England

Printed and bound in England by J.H. Haynes & Co. Ltd, Sparkford

# Contents

# Freelancers

**ALF ALDERSON**

Alf Alderson is a freelance journalist and photographer based in Pembrokeshire, Wales. He specialises in adventure travel and adventure sports, and is the author of a number of surfing guides and outdoor guides. His work appears in The Guardian, The Independent on Sunday, The Times and other UK and foreign newspapers and magazines.

**JUDY ARMSTRONG**

Judy Armstrong is a New Zealander, now living in North Yorkshire, England. She is an award-winning feature writer, specialising in adventure travel and outdoor pursuits - from ski touring to sea kayaking, mountain biking and walking. She returns regularly to New Zealand and has travelled widely ñ on foot, by horse, bike, boat and bus - through North and South America, Africa, Europe and Asia.

**TOM BAILEY**

Tom has worked as Trail magazineís resident photographer for the past five years, forging for the magazine a unique visual identity. Tomís innovative landscape photography and expressive portraiture have earned him industry-wide respect and a generation of imitators.

**MARK GLAISTER**

Mark Glaister has been Rock-Climbing, Mountaineering and Backpacking since the age of twelve. Now forty-two he has travelled the world pursuing his passion, that to many (none more so than himself) seems to be as strong as ever. Mark has always worked as a freelance writer and photographer and has contributed to magazines world-wide.
His thinking behind each of his features is that they should be the sort of article that HE would pay good money to read.

**JOSEP PEREZ GONZALEZ**

Josep Perez Gonzalez uses his work as a photographer as an extension to his primary occupation as a filmmaker. He is based in Barcelona and produced and directed his first short-movie in 1994.
He has always felt a special attraction to the wild landscape and found that photography was the perfect complement to his job.

**TOM HUTTON**

It took Tom Hutton over 20 years to realise that he didnít look good in a suit and tie. It then took him less than 30 seconds to hand in his notice.
Since then, his photography has won him awards and his appetite for adventure has taken him all over the world.
Heís passionate about wild places and also a very keen naturalist. He lives in Wales with his partner, Steph, and 2 Labradors, Honey and India.

**NIGEL JENKINS**

Nigel Jenkins is currently working in Bangalore, India, as a professional engineer. He has been trekking and climbing for the past 15 years on 5 different continents, and has been writing and taking photographs for the past decade.
His works generally centres on landscapes and local people, and his written work attempts to capture the flavour of the trip and the characters encountered.

**ED KENYON**

Ed is a former editor of Trail magazine who has traveled Europe and beyond on the company credit card. He continues to work in the outdoors media business, as publisher of Country Walking, Bird Watching and Trail.

**GUY PROCTER**

Guy is the editor of Trail magazine. Dividing his time between homes in Peterborough and Cortina d'Ampezzo, he is a confirmed via ferrata and long distance path nut. Resident in Hong Kong until the age of 12 he spent much of his early life aboard his father's sloop, the Tangerine Dream, where a lifelong love of terra firma was born. He has two children and an Enfield Bullet, with all three of whom he hopes one day to cross the Himalaya.

**MATTHEW ROBERTS**

Matthew Roberts has been a photographer for 15 years. He specialises in outdoor sports and pursuits including hill walking, horses, mountain biking for leading national magazines. These subjects take him from one end of the UK to the other and also abroad. The magazines demand a high level of creativity and call for various disciplines which include landscapes, portraiture, sports action and still life.

**BRIAN SCHOFIELD**

Brian Schofield is the editor of the Sunday Times Travel Magazine.
He began his career as staff writer on Trail, before moving into an award-winning travel writing career, working for GQ, Arena, the New Statesman and others.
Deep down, he wishes he was still working at Trail!

**WENDY TEASDILL**

Wendy Teasdill lived abroad for many years, teaching English in the cities of the world, walking in remote places and meditating on time concepts. She has published two books: Walking to the Mountain, an account of a lone trek across Western Tibet to Mount Kailash (Asia 2000, 1996) and Yoga for Pregnancy (Gaia Books, 2000).
Now a yoga teacher living in Glastonbury with her three children, she continues to write, particularly about Tibet, Yoga and the strange twists which connect time with eternity.

**MARTIN VARLEY**

Martin Varley is trained as an environmental scientist with 10 years experience of writing and photographing the outdoors.
He specialises in conservation and countryside issues in the UK and overseas and is a member of the Outdoor Writers Guild.
He is based in Kendal, Cumbria, and lives with his wife and two children.

**CHRISTIAN WALSH**

Christian Walsh is a British travel journalist, photographer and Lonely Planet author. He has hiked extensively in South America, Asia, Europe and North Africa.
Based in London he writes freelance features for The Independent, The Times and numerous other publications and websites. You can view his online portfolio at www.christianwalsh.com.

**JASPER WINN**

Jasper Winn is a writer, photographer, radio documentary maker and horseman. For twenty years he has journeyed on foot - as well as by horse, kayak, bicycle and camel - to research the lives and traditions of those people who still work and travel in the world's remoter regions. He has made long journeys with Berber tribes, South American vaqueros, Tuareg and Australian cattle drovers. His travels have taken him to the Sahara, across Patagonia, through Iranian tribal areas, far into the Outback and above the Arctic Circle.

**BEN WINSTON**

From an unpromising start in the depths of a Dartmoor bog, Ben Winston has gone on to become a keen walker, climber and mountaineer. Enjoying nothing more than time in the hills, he combined this outdoor passion with writing and photography to produce some of the features in this book. Now working for publications including Trail and the Independent on Sunday, plus feature's agency Real Vision, he divides his time between the UK and various hot, steamy or hilly countries abroad. He is also working on his first book.

# Foreword by
# GUY PROCTER

**N**ot many of us find the time to learn the language of the countries to which we travel. It's a shame, but luckily that's not the only way of getting under another nation's skin. The other option is to walk it; leave the homogenous world of international brands and motorised travel behind and set foot on the naked rock, turf or snow of another culture. Metered at the steady pace of walking, sights, sounds and smells infuse gradually – instead of a confusing blur, walking renders foreign landscapes intelligible. It also makes us more intelligible to the people we meet. After all, we all know how it feels to travel on foot. Arrive in a mountain village at the end of a long day's walk and you've got the international language of tired feet, sun-burnt features and rumbling stomach with which to break the ice.

This book is about exploring the world on your own two feet. From the laddered heights of the Dolomites to the Nyika Plateau of Malawi, the playground of the Pyrenees to the eerie heights of Tibet, the best of the world is best enjoyed on foot. The articles gathered here are designed to point you in the right direction; to inspire and inform and let you discover the power of pedestrian travel for yourself.

# SHE PAID £42 TO GET HERE

...AND SHE DIDN'T NEED A MONTH OFF WORK EITHER.
THANKS TO THE MAGIC OF THE BUDGET AIRLINE AGE,
YOU TOO CAN WALK THE EPIC GR5.

Words & photographs **Brian Schofield**

**Q**uit the job, ditch the spouse, have the cat put down, invite some gypsies to move into the garden and leave a brief note for the milkman – "Gone to walk across Europe – it's just over 1,200 miles; see you in 18 months, when I'll weigh around four stone and have linoleum for skin."

That's about the ridiculously long and short of tackling a classic path in full. I mean, from Mexico to Canada one step at a time, from Brussels to Istanbul at 14 miles a day? Epic trekking is a noble pursuit, and no doubt hugely rewarding, but having a job can be vaguely rewarding too, and a relationship and a family are not without their merits, which means there has to be some compromise. The path might go on forever, but maybe I don't want to.

In the far southern Alps this is the sort of ridge-walking you do all day.

As far as the great paths of Europe are concerned, that compromise has, in recent years, become much easier to reach. Because now the map of our continent is, in the trail-walker's mind, decorated with two vital tracings. In one colour, there have always been the twisty, coast- and mountain-hugging lines of the long paths – each one taunting you to 'walk me next year, then me the year after, then me!' But now there are the second, equally tempting, route-marks – those magical big bendy arrows that tell you where the budget airlines land, making a weekend in Stockholm less stressful than a trip to the Croydon Ikea. Combine the two maps, and you're onto something – long-distance walking in short-haul chunks, with the attendant simplicity and cost of a holiday, not a mid-life crisis. And where the lines cross and cross again, and the options for getting there pile higher than the hills, you've probably found the GR5 – the ultimate convenience trek.

The full Grand Randonée 5 runs from Belgium to the Med, but the action really starts when the path adopts a more ambitious moniker – La Grande Traversée des Alpes Françaises, and heads almost due south from Lac Leman over almost 400 miles of valleys and high passes to Nice. You could do that route in about five weeks, and spend the rest of the year staring out of the office window thinking about it; or you could take advantage of the path's links to Geneva airport, Nice airport, Lyon airport, Grenobles airport and the sleeper train from Paris, and thus cut the challenge into more chunks than a vat of Sheba.

My bespoke tailoring trimmed the GR5 down to three weeks – the 190-mile stretch from Pralognan-la-Vanoise to Nice, hopefully taking in the southbound transition from high-Alpine trekking to olive-grove sloth. Harriet, my immeasurably better half, took responsibility for accommodation and provisions, while I agreed to handle equipment and navigation – secretly satisfied that I got the better deal.

### DAY 1

So far, everything has gone swimmingly, apart from the equipment and the navigation. The journey from carousel to trolley is enough to demonstrate that our efforts at packing light were not stringent enough, and we'll have to shed weight fast. Meanwhile, Pralognan, our starting point, isn't proving as accessible as I planned – three trains and a bus eventually

Marmots – you either love them or hate them.

deliver us at dusk, only to find (sweet triumph!) that Harriet has mistakenly booked a refuge five miles up the valley. Another bed is found, and solace swiftly reached in the discovery that French home cooking is at its best in the mountains – up here, the trickery of sauces and sautées is mixed with the more urgent functions of mountain grub, to warm, to fill, to cheer. And up here, joyously, the cream, the butter, the eggs, the cheese, they don't count as Gallic decadence – they're fuel!

### DAY 2

Our very first splash of red and white paint points through the trees and into the widening, cloud-smothered bowl of the Chavière valley, where a casting seems to be taking place for *The Life of Mammals*. "Look! I can't believe we've seen a marmot on our very first morning! And another! And…oh, I see, they're absolutely everywhere...." *Bouquetins* (ibex), the bulky goats with horns like rugby posts, are slightly less ubiquitous than the rodent bulldogs at our feet, but they still pose willingly for the camera and we continue a perfect opening day, gaining height towards our first mountain pass, pausing only to visit a refuge and share The Finest Omelette in History.

### DAY 3

Harriet wants to go home. I don't blame her. We've just descended 1700m without pause, from the befogged Col de Chavière to the utterly miserable train-stop town of Modane. Both of us have knees like pink grapefruit and backs like Albert Steptoe's, and our morale lights are flickering red. Thank God, there's a post office, from which to send home a brutal cull of any excess baggage – "I'll use your toothbrush from now on; I'll imagine a novel," – and there's the inspiration of meeting a solo lady GR5-er from Harrogate, who's devouring the miles on just a tin of peas, some mackerel and a handful of dried fruit a day. Armed with rubbed-off British pluck, we rest, and forge on.

### DAY 8

I doze on a bench outside, watching the paragliders and trying to stay calm while the Ceillac village doctor laconically (I assume) decides the fate of our holiday. In the last four days we've crossed more spectacular mountain scenery than you'd imagine could be walked through in a month, and we've settled into the peaceful, welcoming routine of the mountain refuges at night, but while my knees have slowly recovered from the descent into Modane, Harriet's have got steadily more niggly. In the end, medical advice was the only grown-up option.

The grin, on emergence, says it all, The conversation has gone as follows: "You're doing the GR5?" Yes. "You haven't trained enough?" Maybe. "You want to continue?" Yes. "Take these."
Cue handover of a box of drugs sufficient to stop the swelling that would occur if you were released naked into Space. "Now enjoy the walk, and make sure you use the trekking poles. Goodbye."

# This is a National Park that really means it – no campsites, no developments, no new roads, no nothing

View, what a scorcher!
At Lac Saint-Anne in the Queyras
region, with the temperature
hitting 30 degrees.

Glass act: the obviously named Lac Miroir.

Marmite (or is it marmot?) and tuna sandwiches – of course!

Ceillac is beautiful and perfectly positioned for circular walks through the towering Queyras range, but we have to move on – doctor's orders.

### DAY 13
A rest day in Saint Etienne de Tinée, and not a moment too soon – not out of exhaustion but from the need to take it all in. The crossing of the Haute Alpes from Ceillac has been a gluttonous binge of Alpine experiences, starting with the perfect sheen of the Lac Mirour, the film-devouring wonder of Lac Saint-Anne, the silent, nervous zigzag to the fading views of ever, ever more mountains from the Col Giradin, and finally the first encounter with the star of the show – the Mercantour. This is a National Park that really means it – no campsites, no developments, no new roads, no nothing. And the reward for the puritanism is purity, a sensation you don't fully get at any other point on the route – that you're not safely in the cradle of civilisation, that you're not two hours from a warm village, that you're in a place, in western Europe, where real, wild wolves can hide. After we've crossed the Mercantour via the Pas de Cavalle and settled into the most ancient and rickety of all the mountain huts we've stayed in, at the tiny summer hamlet of Bousiéyas, I categorically name my 'best day of the trip' and my ambition for 2003 – the (bivvy-only) Tour of the Mercantour. But for now, a day of rest and café culture is all we need, before what is hopefully the gentle downhill stretch to Nice.

### DAY 14
A brief pastoral lesson. If you're going to be a shepherd in wolf country, you're going to need more than sheepdogs. You're going to need wolfdogs. Big, hairy, long-toothed beasts than can come out ahead in a dirty fight with a wolf. You aren't, however (because this is the Mercantour National Park and visitors are pollution), obliged to teach your wolfdog the difference between a wolf and a walker. If you're a walker, the park signs succinctly point out, your only option is to stand dead still until the Hound of Hell barking its face off two feet away from you realises you're not a wolf or, as in our case, you may have to hide in a forest for almost an hour while

the sun sets, until the dog gets bored of you. Here endeth.

### DAY 17
The Alpes Maritimes, the supposed dying embers of the Alps as they slip into the sea, have proved to be nothing like the stroll we expected. The diminishing gradient is balanced by marathon gaps between suitable accommodation, and we sample our first 12-hour day, now attended by a full-beam Mediterranean sun. The rewards are the shifting views, with pine forests and escarpments giving the feeling we've moved to Corsica in the night, and when we pass through beech forests, the feel of leaves crunching beneath our caked boots. I've never walked through the seasons before.

### DAY 19
The sea! I can see the sea!! Harriet, agonisingly, refuses to believe me, but I can see the sea. Just above the lights of that town, where the land gets hazy, there it is. I think. Maybe. Oh, I don't know.

### DAY 20
Our final early morning – starting at dawn has been the one aspect of this trip that has categorically not been in the holiday spirit – and a short walk from the beautiful hilltop town of Aspremont secures an agreed first sighting of the Mediterranean. From here we gradually return to humanity, from the parks to the suburbs to the centre of Nice, and are suitably confused by the time we collapse at the finish line – the beach.

It's probably a measure of the depth of the experience that three weeks in the solitude and natural blessedness of the High Alps brings, that neither of us feel capable of functioning even in this most civilised of cities. It's a measure of the extraordinary, 21st century ease of the experience that all we have to do now is walk down the perfectly named Promenade des Anglais and get on a bus to the airport. The trip of a lifetime, just a few mouse clicks and a couple of hours away. Sometimes you have to remind yourself how lucky you are.

# The French GR5 in chunks

## 1 WEEK
### LAC LÉMAN TO CHAMONIX
We started too far south to be able to vouch personally for this trip, but by all reports it's a stunner. Fly to Geneva and catch the train to Montreux, then a steamboat, of all things, to St. Gingolph (or a taxi if you've missed the sailing). It's five or six days through ever-steepening mountains to Les Houches, and the train back to Geneva .

## 2 WEEKS
### CHAMONIX VALLEY TO MODANE
A leisurely-paced two weeks (make sure you don't arrive early in the charmless Modane). Fly to Geneva then catch the train to St. Gervais. You'll need to follow the full GR5 route through the Vanoise, and take a rest day in the lonely Pralognan-la-Vanoise. From Modane, it's a direct train to Lyon, and home.

## 2 WEEKS
### MODANE TO ST ETIENNE DE TINÉE
Possibly the best fortnight in the Alps. Fly to Lyon and take the train to Modane, From there it's 10 days of walking through the Haute Alpes. You might need the rest days – best spent in the priceless Ceillac. Catch the early morning bus to Nice from St Etienne and fly home.

## 1 WEEK
### ST ETIENNE DE TINÉE TO NICE
Get a return ticket to Nice (Easyjet flies from Liverpool, East Midlands, Bristol, Luton, Stansted and Gatwick, www.easyjet.com 0870 600 0000) and catch the bus up the hills to St Etienne (twice a day, contact Riviera Tourism for details 0033 493 377878). From here it's fascinating six days though the Mediterranean Alps back to the big city, and home. Not a rugged Alpine experience, and less bounteous accommodation, but a taste of a very different France.

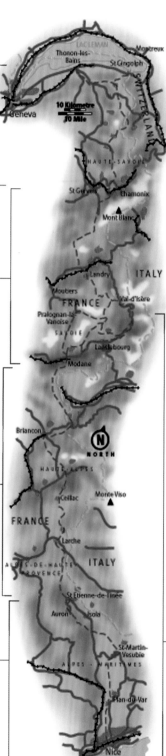

## 4-5 DAYS
### CHAMONIX VALLEY TO LANDRY
Fly to Geneva and catch to train to St. Gervais for the Chamonix valley. Walk for four days through the lonely Beaufortain and stunning Tarentaise regions to Landry, and either catch the sleeper train back to Paris or change trains at Moutiers for Geneva and get your return flight home.

## 4-5 DAYS
### LANDRY TO MODANE
Leave work in time to catch a budget flight or train to Paris. British Airways is currently flying to Paris from UK airports: www.ba.com 0845 779977. Eurostar London Waterloo-Paris: www.raileurope.co.uk 08705 848 848; then overnight sleeper to Landry. Alternatively, fly direct to Geneva (Easyjet goes to Geneva from Liverpool, East Midlands, Luton and Gatwick, return including tax, www.easyjet.com, 0870 600 0000) and catch the train to Landry via a change at Moutiers. Walk for four days through some of the highest and wildest terrain on the whole Alpine route, following the GR55 variant on the path to ensure you reach Modane in good time to catch the train direct to Lyon for budget flight home (Easyjet, flies Lyon to Stansted).

## 3 WEEKS
### PRALOGNAN LA-VANOISE TO NICE
Our itinerary, and a tricky start, catching the train from Geneva airport to Moutiers and the twice-daily bus to Pralognan (contact Rhone-Alpes Tourisme, 0033 472 592159), followed by a tough two days to Modane. But from there on it's an awesome tour south through the changing, warming Alps. To possibly improve the trip you could start at Modane and take the spare days to explore the Mercantour Park or the area around Ceillac, or alternatively start a week higher north, in Landry, and get the bus to Nice from St Etienne de Tinée – but nothing beats the first view of the sea. Fly home from Nice.

Illustration: Jeremy Ashcroft

---

# Fact file

A CICERONE GUIDE
**WALKING THE**
**FRENCH ALPS: GR5**
MARTIN COLLINS

## WHEN TO GO
The ideal time is from the end of August until the first two weeks of October, when the crowds are gone and the clouds are more stable. You could also consider mid-May until mid-July, but you should be aware of the likelihood of encountering snow on the high passes. If at all possible, avoid the mid-July to August madness – or you'll spend some nights sleeping in corridors, on tables or in the yard outside, and at least one day beneath a violent thunderstorm.

## EQUIPMENT
The crucial weight-diminishing step is to chuck out your tough, all-season waterproofs and get high-quality lightweight shells. Combined with a good midweight fleece and a long-sleeved top, that's a great bulk-to-warmth balance. The next step is the brave one – throw out the sleeping bag. Provided it's not August, there will be plenty of blankets at every *refuge* and *gîte*, so a cotton or silk liner is all you need. For footwear – this is not the Appalachian Trail: trainers won't cut it, well-loved 3-season boots will. Finally, those epic descents demand trekking poles, and that sun deserves a serious hat. My Driza-Bone waxed cotton titfer, bought for the trip, is fully waterproof and feels like a purchase for life ((020) 7836 2292 www.australiashop.co.uk, prices from £29.95).

## ACCOMMODATION
Beds along the way are plentiful, in Club Alpine Française mountain refuges and privately run hostels called *gîtes d'étapes*, and these establishments are listed in the Cicerone Guide and easily found in the small towns and villages where you'll stop. Expect to pay £5-7 for a bed and £20 for a demi-pension – a hearty dinner, bed and a bread 'n' coffee breakfast. Phoning and reserving a bed is a struggle, but only a necessary evil in August.
For the numbers of every *gîte* and *refuge* in France, get a copy of *Gîtes D'etape et Refuges* by Annick and Serge Mouraret, a resource which could change your life (£24.95 on amazon.co.uk, ISBN 2841821684). If your trip is in the northern half of the Grande Traverse, a British Mountaineering Club refuge card, which gets you a discount at CAF huts, is a worthwhile investment (www.the-bmc.co.uk for details).

## HEALTH & SAFETY
You need to be hill-fit before you start the GR5, if you want to enjoy it. You also need to have been toughening-up your joints, out on the slopes, carrying a pack. Your other chief health concern is dehydration – particularly in the southern Alps, where the running streams start to go missing. Carry rehydration salts as a precaution. Finally, there's the thunderstorms. You could try curling up in a ball with your elbows on the ground when the lightning gets close, but the best defence is an early breakfast and getting off the tops by mid-afternoon.

The excellent Refuge de Maljasset in Chambeyron.

# HUT TO TROT

DON'T LET THE BIG, BAD ALPS PUT YOU OFF. WORD IS THAT A JUICY SECTION OF THE AUSTRIAN TYROL IS TAILOR-MADE FOR UK READERS...

Words Ed Kenyon Photography **Tom Bailey**

A classic Karwendel day – sun, rocky peaks and the thought of apple strudel at the next hut.

Clockwise from left: A taste of Klettersteige. The Lamsenjochhütte dwarfed by the scale of Hochnissl (2547m). Helmet, harness and karabiner cows' tails – essential kit. This way for Austrian hospitality!

As alarm calls go, it was one of the more laid-back varieties. My eyes flickered open and focused on the slats of the bunk above me while my brain played catch-up. The bells tinkled again outside the hut window as the cows continued their breakfast of succulent high Alpine pasture. I wondered whether it was possible to acquire a tasteful cowbell alarm for home, then thought better of it. It was time to get going – the final leg of the Karwendel Tour in Austria's northern Tyrol was beckoning and, loath though I was to leave these magical mountains, we had a rendezvous with a taxi.

Look at a map of Europe and you'll see just how vast the Alps really are. A great swathe of mountain and valley thousands of square kilometres in area – an enormous wealed scar, the result of monumental fisticuffs between the African and European continents about 65 million years ago. But how the hell do you pick where to go walking in all that?!

You can follow the honeypot trails and wonder in awe at the majesty of Mont Blanc et al – along with the coachloads (don't get me wrong, you should do it once); or maybe you could head to the recently in-vogue Eastern European countries (again, don't turn your nose up just because Whymper didn't go playing there in the 19th century).

But what about the vast expanse in between? You can try the old map game of pinning a radio mast on the mountain and go for pot luck, or you can go with personal recommendation. The latter is what I did, and that's what I'm doing for you. I'm no mountain goat with an encyclopaedic knowledge of every Alpine hut; I was merely a UK hill-walker in need of some inspiration – and boy did I get it.

Striding out into the Karwendel on day one, with our lunchtime hut destination perched like an eyrie at the head of the glacially-scoured valley, I knew we'd struck gold. Before this trip I'd never even heard of the Karwendel, and if someone had suggested taking an Alpine walking break on the Austria-German border I'd have said "Nein, danke – give me the Aosta Valley or the Dolomites any day." However, as each stunning mountain scene peeled away to reveal an ever more spectacular one I was scouring my Deutsch-English phrasebook for superlatives.

Lunch at the impressive Karwendelhaus Hut involved *Gulaschsuppe* (thick, spicy soup) and *Knodel* (dumplings) followed by (yes it had to be) *Apfelstrudel*. While I would be lying if I said it was the main reason for coming to the Karwendel, these mountain huts are superb and make the logistics of a trip like this so much more straightforward. They all have mountain vantage points which make the Snowdon café seem like a motorway service station, and bed and board which most Brits would be content with at sea-level, never mind five or six thousand feet above. Hot water, comfy beds, small rooms if required, showers, real toilets (as opposed to mountain long drops where you either pick up hepatitis or splinters) and decent beer. This all means that you can cut down on the weight of your pack. Indeed, for five days' summer walking you shouldn't need anything larger than 35-40 litres.

The main reason why we'd flown to Munich and got a bus to Innsbruck and then Scharnitz where we started, was that we'd been assured this enclave of sharp limestone ridges and peaks was a perfect match for our brand of 'adventurous hill-walking'. Good, hard routes in superb mountain scenery; no snow or glaciers

Clockwise from above: Trail and 'Mountain Mike' toast another great day. "Moo are you looking at?" Crossing the canyon-like Zwerchbach. Easy trekking, Karwendel-style.

thanks (leave crampons etc at home); not heaving with people; throw in a slice of the local *via ferrata* (called *Klettersteige* round here) and the chance to stay high at night was all on our list. After a few days in the Karwendel we'd ticked them all off.

These are serious mountains and, because of the topography, there are some big ascents/descents. But one thing you don't have to worry about – and this is part of its charm – is that nowhere does it creep over the 3000m altitude mark. This means no permanent glaciers and a high point of 2749m – the Birkkarspitze – which is well within the reach of fit hill-walkers.

There's something hugely impressive – in a different way to the traditional snow-covered Alpine peaks – about these vast knife-edge mountain ridges of grey rock. As you head deeper and deeper into their precipitous domain the sheer scale of the big walls and jagged peaks blocks the outside world from your mind. The only things concerning you are "Will there be any apple strudel at the next hut?" and "Why didn't I come here before?"

## the early morning view from 7,000ft was of such rare quality it was worth the air fare alone

The Karwendel trails are well marked and, for the most part, very easy to follow. The high paths are no problem when walked with the very straightforward local maps and there is no shortage of clear reference points, although things can get interesting down in the hidden valleys.

Just as the Karwendel peaks are a contrast to the usual Alpine experience, so are some of the valleys. Combine these two in a day and you have a unique Alpine experience tailor-made for the Trail way of doing things. On probably our hardest day, from the Lamsenjochhütte to the Hallerangerhaus Hut, we tasted the complete Karwendel.

Peering out of our bunk room window we could see the Klettersteige snaking its way up what looked like a near-vertical wall. Mountain Mike, our local mountain goat, er, guide, geared us up at the bottom and shot off up the route like a chamois up a couloir. There was nothing to fear – the cable was good and strong, the holds plentiful and the early morning view from 7,000ft of such rare quality it was worth the air fare alone.

Having no shame, and making a clear distinction between actual rock-climbing and Klettersteige, we used every available rung and piton to hoist our way ever higher, emerging onto the ridge through a cave-like hole which had no logical right to be where it was.

All around us the rock architecture pierced the sky and, even though we were only 15km from Innsbruck, the modern world could not penetrate our reverie. A few swigs of water and Mike was off, using his poles expertly as we dropped down and down, first zigzagging and then full-on off-piste scree-running. Somehow our knees coped with 1300m of descent in only 2km. As we drank deeply from the clear, cold mountain stream it felt as if we were at the bottom of the world.

We saw only four people all day as we traversed our way along the valley bottom, mindful of the potentially fatal drop into the river below. Everywhere was the reminder of flood damage with full-size trees strewn like discarded matches along the river banks. Waterfalls cascaded on all sides. The long walk-out was draining in the high humidity and we felt like true pioneers, hemmed in on either side by rows of impenetrable 2600m peaks.

Eventually, with fading legs (extra choc/energy bars are essential) we crested the Uberschalljoch saddle and gaped at a mountain vista so impressive we felt certain God was considering

membership of the Alpine Club when he designed this. The Hallerangerhaus Hut stood perched at the end of a hanging valley with front row seats to a showing of some of the Karwendel's finest peaks. Huge, sheer big walls, rose up from the valley floor and the mountains curved round like a giant horseshoe, offering only a glimpse of what could be the way out.

Over an enormous meal and one too many beers Mike regaled us with tales of his Karwendel climbs, snowstorms in summer and how the Austrians really are different to the Germans. But as we sauntered out the following morning accompanied by the gentle ringing of the cowbells, I realised that you don't need a guide to be able to enjoy the delights of the Karwendel. Hire one if you're up for some *Klettersteige*; otherwise buy a map, follow the trails and have yourself an Alpine experience like no other.

# Fact file

## WHY GO?
- Superb rock architecture
- Well-marked trails
- No need for crampons or axes
- No altitude worries
- Great hut network
- The perfect 'Alpine experience'
- The apple strudel

## DO
Book the huts in advance via Tyrol Tourist Board – see right for details
**Learn a smattering of German before you go – more for politeness than necessity**
Take extra choc/snack supplies as the packed lunches are spartan
**Give yourself at least one night at the end in a comfy hotel in somewhere like Seefeld – your aches will diminish and you can soak up the Austrian hospitality**
Take plenty of water bottles – it can get very hot in summer and there is often no water to be had in between huts
**Use trekking poles – your knees will thank you for it**
Take sleeping bag liner for the huts (you don't need a bag)
**Pack hut slippers or sandals**
Remember 3-4 season boots if you're going to do a *Klettersteige*. Take decent 3-season boots otherwise
**Sample jugs of *Radler* in the huts (an Austrian lager-top, very refreshing)**

## DON'T
Forget your sun cream
**Underestimate the height gains/drop between huts**
Take too much kit (warm fleece, hut slippers/sandals and mountain waterproofs are all the extras you need)
**Try the *Klettersteige* unless you are properly protected and either have a guide or are climbing with an experienced partner**

## THE KARWENDEL ROUND
Because of the good hut network and excellent rail and road links around the Karwendel, you can make up your own route. However, as a general rule of thumb, because of the vast ridge lines running west-east, the walking is easier in these directions. North-south walking will involve a lot more ascent/descent.

There is a leaflet (in German, but it gives you the daily breakdowns on the map) available from the Tyrol Tourist Board, detailing The Karwendel Round. This starts at Seefeld (picturesque ski resort town) and heads east via the Nordlinger Hut-Solsteinhaus-Seegrubbe-Pfeishutte-Hallerangerhaus before finishing at Scharnitz. You then get a bus back to Seefeld.

Our guide devised a slightly different version which started and finished at Scharnitz and went via Karwendelhaus-Falkenhutte (for lunch!)-Lamsenjochhutte-Hallerangerhaus.

This is a 3-4 day trip.
Alternatively you can do a straightforward west-east traverse from Scharnitz to Schwaz with a train at either end. This six -day trip is covered in detail in *Walking Austria's Alps Hut to Hut* by Jonathan Hurdle.

All of these are fantastic trips; just pick the one which best suits your time requirements or make up your own from the network of huts.

## HOW TO GET THERE
You can fly direct to Innsbruck which is only a short taxi ride to Seefeld or Scharnitz, the traditional starts of the Karwendel but it isn't cheap as yet. There is talk of a budget airline heading this way soon but for the moment it's scheduled which means fares start from about £170 return – see www.flights4less.com

Munich is cheaper with Easyjet (www.easyjet.com). From Munich you can get a bus to Innsbruck and on to Seefeld or Scharnitz or a train – see www.europeonrail.com for details.

## TOURIST INFO
The Tyrol Tourist Board and the local offices will be happy to help with any aspect of your holiday arrangements. They can sort your transport from the airport, book the huts and a guide if required and any other accommodation. For more details contact TLR:
Tiroler Landes Reisebüro
Klosterstrasse 43, A-6100 Seefeld
phone: 0043 5212 2313
fax: 0043 5212 3355
email: info@seefeld.tirol.at
www.seefeld-tirol.com

## FIVE STEPS TO A UNIQUE KARWENDEL EXPERIENCE
1 Book your flights to Munich or Innsbruck – www.easyjet.com or www.flights4less.com
2 Arrange transport to Seefeld or Scharnitz (tourist board can help)
3 Book huts and accommodation via the tourist board
4 Book a guide if you want to try the excellent *Klettersteige*
5 Arrange time off from work and order your euros!

**WHEN TO GO**
Most of the huts are open from June to the middle of October. Avoid August if you can as the heat can be oppressive and the huts busy. Early July and September are good times.

Look after those lugholes!

"Okay, who's buying the ice cream?"

# LADDERED HEIGHTS

ITALY'S DOLOMITES ARE HOME TO A PLAYGROUND OF
SHEER ROCK FACES THAT EVEN YOUR GRAN COULD CLIMB.

Words Alf Alderson Photography **Alf Alderson/Tom Bailey**

Impregnable? Actually, no.
A via ferrata can take you there.

The vie ferrate of the Italian Dolomites are an absolute must for budding mountaineers who can't be bothered with learning all the technical jiggery-pokery of ropes, belays and bits of clanking metal. If you're looking for a full-on, high exposure mountain experience next summer then put this region at the top of your list.

However, when you get there and crane your neck upwards to view the stupendous vertical limestone peaks and towers of the Dolomites you'll convince yourself that their massive walls are off-limits to all but Spiderman, sports climbers and chamois. But look closely and you may spot tiny figures effortlessly ascending these gargantuan rock walls.

These small, multi-coloured dots are scrambling up a *via ferrata*, an 'iron way' on which ordinary mortals can enjoy as much excitement in the mountains as they'll ever have while fully clothed. These sensational scrambles provide access to wild, exposed and very high cliff faces along exhilarating high-level routes that even a complete newcomer to the mountains can enjoy – as my girlfriend was about to discover. But more of that later...

Many of the first *vie ferrate* were constructed between 1915-17 when Italian and Austrian troops tussled for control of the region, and some of these can still be visited today. Thousands of men lived, excavated, tunnelled and died in this beautiful region, some even living in the tunnels and caves of an 'Ice City' beneath the Marmolada Glacier which flows down the slopes of 3344m Marmolada Peak, the highest mountain in the region. Indeed, vie ferrate here take you through the scene of much of the military action.

Further development of the vie ferrate came from the 1930s onwards as more acrobatic members of the Club Alpino Italiano and other local climbing clubs attached wire ropes and iron pegs, rungs and ladders to scores of rock faces throughout the Dolomites. The routes they created, varying from easy traverses to phenomenally exposed vertical crags, give you a relatively safe and easy taste of the

adrenaline-charged world of big face climbing without the need for the technical ability and muscles of the experts (who can often be seen on ironware-free crags in the vicinity).

The enormous blocks of limestone that make up the peaks of the Dolomites are awe-inspiring whether you view them from their summits or their bases. Enormous crags seem almost to burst from the Earth's surface, rising up into Alpine-blue skies in huge sugarloafs, impossibly-serrated needles and vast molar-shaped blocks that, in the light of dawn and dusk especially, are surely some of the most gorgeous mountains on the planet.

Sasshonger, a 2625m peak above our base in the rapidly but tastefully expanding resort of Corvara, is a classic example, standing guard above the northern end of the town, seemingly inaccessible. "Not so," says Maurizio Roveri, a personable mountain guide with whom we'd wandered through the forests, alpine pastures and Great War trenches beneath the Passi de Campolongo the day before.

"Children can climb it. OK, it's a little steep at the top, but you should be fine." Maurizio's words of reassurance were for the benefit of my girlfriend Fiona, whom I'd dragged along on her first-ever visit to 'real' mountains. However, being Irish, she was ready to have a go at anything. And anyway, when a waiter and the hotel receptionist also casually remarked on the ease of ascending Sasshonger despite its forbidding appearance, Anglo-Irish pride left us with little choice but to head for the hill. So on a hot and sunny September morning we set off for the 1100m climb to the top.

The mountain rises steeply from ski slopes, emerald green in late summer; and the higher you climb, the more dramatic becomes the path carved into the glaring white limestone crags. But for all the drama there was no real danger other than from sweating to death; and, as Maurizio had predicted, even the steep final rib of rock was little more than a fun scramble. It was made all the more easy by the presence of a steel hawser you can grab onto for additional security, thus categorising this

## THE GREAT WAR IN THE DOLOMITES

Cynics will love the Dolomites for their proof of mankind's ability to fight over anything – even barren, snow-capped mountains. From 1915 to 1917 the Alpine corps of the Italian and Austrian armies developed systems of tunnels, defences and footpaths through the Dolomites in a bid to gain strategic control of the region. Twenty thousand or more soldiers are thought to have died in the battles, often in rather bizarre ways. For example, in 1916, on the Col di Lana, south-east of Corvara, Italian troops spent months tunnelling into a mountain occupied by Austrian troops before blowing up the entire mountain top, Austrians and all. In 1917 Austrian troops tunnelled under snow on the Sasso di Sesto east of Cortina d'Ampezzo to attack their enemy. And hundreds if not thousands of soldiers on both sides were killed by avalanches and rock falls – some acts of God, others deliberately instigated by mortar shelling.

**For more information on the Great War and the various museums and battlefield sites, log on to www.grandeguerra.dolomiti.org**

Sheer rock face? No problem!

All you have to do is hook up and go.

A bird's-eye view is available to all.

"Technically... it's little harder than climbing up a ladder to clean your bathroom windows..."

last section as a Grade A *via ferrata*, where A is easiest and G hardest.

The views from the summit are ample payback for the loss of buckets of sweat. Way below, Corvara goes about its daily business; across the Val di Corvara is the barren, desert-like hanging valley of the Val de Mesdi, hemmed in by enormous rock towers; and to the south-east are the blue-white slopes of the Marmolada Glacier. While I took in the view through a film of perspiration, Fiona stood on the summit, arms in the air, celebrating an impressive start to her mountaineering career.

A couple of days later we found ourselves clambering into climbing harnesses and clipping onto the rope of mountain guide Giorgio Manica to scramble up the Via Ferrata Brigata Trentina (named after soldiers from Trentino region who helped set up the route). This would be a rather more serious undertaking than Sasshonger, with around 550m of aided climbing graded D, but with a former member of the Italian climbing team in charge we were in safe hands.

Giorgio, a quiet man with an elegance and grace of movement we couldn't hope to emulate, told me that the ironware is inspected regularly by mountain guides – "sometimes I will come up myself and replace it in spring or autumn" - and later, as we climbed, I noticed that he regularly checked the solidity of rungs and hawser anchors. As we shuffled for space among other via ferrata-ists at the bottom of the crag, Giorgio also pointed out that this was quiet compared to August. I know we shouldn't indulge in racial stereotyping in this day and age, but it was noticeable how the German climbers were happy to barge past everyone, the Italians spent as much time gabbing as climbing, and the few Brits on the mountain almost fell off in their eagerness to avoid getting in anyone's way...

"It's best to visit in July or now, September," Giorgio explained. "This time of year there aren't so many people on the mountain – but don't worry, tomorrow I'll take you to a much quieter route."

Within a few metres of starting this ascent of the huge north flank of the Sella Massif you get a taste of the whole via ferrata

The rewards are many.

It's not cheating, honest...

Sasshonger: kids can climb it.

23

Hell hole? Defensive tunnel beneath Tofana di Rozes near Cortina.

experience, first clipping your karabiner into a steel cable bolted at short regular intervals to the rock face, then above this ascending a series of iron rungs set into the rock, beside which another steel cable provides protection.

This was Fiona's first taste of mountain scrambling and climbing, and after the first steep pitches I asked how she was getting on. "Away with yer, boy – I'm having a grand time," came her reply, which just goes to prove that on the easier and middling grade routes anyone who doesn't suffer from vertigo and has a sense of adventure owes it to themselves to have a go.

The Trentina route has a couple of sections towards the top where you're very much exposed to the long, long drop to the valley several hundred metres below, and it's no place to discover you're scared of heights. Technically, though, it's little harder than climbing up a ladder to clean your bathroom windows. But by the time you've scrambled above the waterfall tumbling down from the Lago Pisciadu, up to the very steep and extremely exposed final ascent and across a rocking and rolling suspension bridge traversing a deep, dark canyon, you'll feel the strain on your arms and legs.

And having said how easy it all is, it's worth considering the adventures that two English guys we'd met the day before were getting themselves into as we cruised up the Trentina. Sam and Fergy, outdoor instructors from Yorkshire, were, in their own words, "having a bit of an epic" on the Bec de Mesdi above the Marmolada Glacier. The guide book description as 'interesting' should perhaps act as a warning that this Grade F climb may offer

a challenge or two, but throw in rain, sleet and snow at an altitude of almost 3000m and it's no wonder they were both knackered by the time they finished. The harder vie ferrate should not be undertaken too lightly!

Next morning we awoke to mist in the valley while the sun-tinged upper slopes of the Dolomites rose proud above into a clear blue sky. Fiona had hurt her knee on the descent of the Trentino route the day before, so Giorgio and I were left to tackle 2908m Piz da Lec alone. The start of this relatively short (240m) via ferrata is easily accessed via ski lifts and we managed it in an hour. Mind you, the guidebook recommends 2½ hours; and if I hadn't been sprint-climbing to keep up with Giorgio I would undoubtedly have been nearer this time. Despite being graded D, the same as yesterday's route, this was much more challenging with some technically difficult moves where rock-climbing skills were required. We also had to negotiate a vertigo-inducing face towards the summit, via iron ladders so close to vertical I swear they were overhanging.

It was unfortunate that as we'd gone up the clouds had come down and hidden the spectacular view across Val de Mesdi and the Sella Massif, one of the main reasons for doing this climb. No matter; I'd had the excitement of my third via ferrata and was already hooked and planning next year's trip. A full year leaves me plenty of time to hone my rope and knot work, which is close to useless. But maybe I won't bother. You see, one of the beauties of the via ferrata is that you don't need to be a rope master to crack it.

# Fact file

### GETTING THERE
From the south of England it's as easy to get to the Dolomites as to Scotland. And the weather is a lot better. And there are no midges! Inghams Lakes & Mountains offers a wide choice of package deals in the Italian Dolomites, and we stayed with them at the 3-star Hotel Marmolada in Corvara. To book call Inghams reservation line – tel. (020) 8780 4433, or visit www.inghams.co.uk

### EQUIPMENT
Essential equipment includes a climbing harness, about 3.5m of 11mm rope, two special via ferrata self-locking karabiners with rope blocks, a kinetic impact shock absorber and a climbing helmet.
Local climbing shops sell the full rig (apart from helmet). It's simple to use, but if in doubt consider employing a guide for the day and you'll quickly pick up the technique to enable you to go solo.
To hire a guide contact Associazione Guide Alpine Val Badia, Str. Col Alt 36, 39033, Corvara (BZ) – tel. 0039 0471 836898, or e-mail guide.valbadia@rolmail.net

### INFORMATION
Via Ferrata – Scrambles in the Dolomites translated by Cecil Davies, pb Cicerone £12.99 is an essential English language guide featuring almost 90 routes. Also contact Corvara Tourist Information Office at the above address – tel. 0039 0471 836176, e-mail corvara@altbadia.org For more information on the Alta Badia region and the routes described above, log onto www.altabadia.org

# GET SOME THERAPY!

WANT TO BEAT STRESS, GET FIT AND DISCOVER A LASTING SENSE OF HAPPINESS?
THEN ENROL IN A TWO-WEEK PROGRAMME THAT'S GOOD FOR THE SOUL...

Words and photography **Ben Winston**

Clean air, sunshine and steely-blue tarns at Circ de Colomers high in the Pyrenees: the sort of stuff that keeps you sane.

What would you say to a revolutionary new health programme that promised total fitness, mental clarity, sharpened senses and increased confidence in just two weeks? For the price of a short flight and a fortnight's food, you could reap rewards that self-help books, aromatherapy and primal screaming sessions can only dream of. You'd have the freedom to do whatever you wanted, whenever you wanted to do it, in a completely stress-free environment. Well, that programme does exist and it works. All it takes is two weeks, one rucksack and a few very large mountains...

When we set out for a couple of weeks in the Pyrenees with a few hundred miles in mind, it was simply a holiday. We weren't searching for salvation or enlightenment, or to find that 'inner me'. We were just walking, realising a long-promised dream to spend some quality time in one of Europe's greatest ranges. As it happened we chose Spain's GR11 route in late season, partly for the fact we could book cheap flights to nearby Barcelona and partly because all the other tourists would have gone home. To be honest, we could have chosen any of the many GR routes that criss-cross

the range. The essentials – and the rewards – would have been the same: time out in the wilderness and the emergence of a relaxed human being from his festering trench of stress.

We started our route in the smog-free, traffic jam-free, tax-free wonderland of Andorra. It was there we remembered that before any extended time away from supermarkets and 24-hour garages, a certain amount of preparation is required. Shopping. Food. Blister kits. Indispensable things such as maps. So, next morning, flanked by bemused Andorran window shoppers, two large rucksacks with legs waddled round hunting for essentials.

In the supermarket things got a little heated as each product was tested against our criteria: low weight, high nutrition and great taste, plus how much of it we would need for the next fortnight. We ended up thinking of food in terms of fuel, searching for the most combustible mix of calories, carbohydrates and proteins. By the time we left, our rucksacks were knobbled with packs of pasta and our legs had assumed the bowed position of old age. When we climbed into the minibus, it groaned audibly.

As a result, the memory of that first day will stay with me

Refreshing spring water cascades over rocks.

Climbing up the high pass Port de Ratera, we realise we're fitter than we thought.

assume it's sausage.

The Sound of Moosic?

Catch up on some Mick Brown.

But what's on the other side..?

GR11 route markings.

Even the slow worms chill out.

forever: plodding up from the road and away from civilisation, leaving behind us the brown hazy valleys where a thousand duty-free evils beckoned. It was one of those hellish mornings beset by self-doubt and aching muscles. It felt like an enforced banishment from the comforts of the world – a form of unremitting purgatory. Sweat itched, straps and buckles rubbed and the next two weeks looked less like a holiday and more like an army training course. But we climbed and climbed, struggling on quietly, battling with fatigue and worrying about our slow pace and the distance we had to cover to the nearest mountain hut before nightfall. And then, by lunchtime, we collapsed by a stream, pretty much spent.

And it was there beside that stream that, for the first time, we realised where we were.

Down the valley the trees stretched away in wave after wave of slow-turning gold, some keener than others for autumn. Above, where the tree line faded to scrub and rocks, stood the mountains. Yet it wasn't the scenery that sliced through the malcontent of our efforts, but the tinkling of the stream, the eddies and bubbles and crazy-coursed leaves negotiating the rapids. It was the ant that got itself half drowned and struggled with a tenuous, one-legged grasp on the dry rock; its efforts at heaving itself to safety and its unwillingness to give up before I intervened. It was the flicker of a wren, the freshness of the air, the slow-moving arc of the sun. It was an eagle soaring on thermals we couldn't see. In fact, it was everything that was wild and natural, everything that wasn't man-made or constrained by human boundaries – international borders, the time, day, month or year. It was the dawning realisation that we were, for the first time in what felt like years, totally and utterly free.

And when, later that day, we crossed into Spain, it was without fanfare or passport control. The plants and birds showed little regard for the border too. And, when we stopped for the night – in a strange metal hut – it was not because we had to rush home in time for supper, but simply because we were exhausted and it was dark. So we wrapped ourselves up warm in the musty blankets provided in the bivouac and cooked a roaring supper by the light of the candles. Outside in the moonlight, a crisp frost settled in the hollows and crawled up over the peaks.

The next day the novelty of such a sheer lack of responsibility was still fresh. We woke late and cooked a rank breakfast of soup and small, star-shaped pasta – the sort of thing that looks and tastes superb in the hills but resembles nothing so much as vomit below the 1500m contour. As we were cooking in the warmth of the sun, a small, wiry and aged Canadian man popped up from behind a rock, and stopped to cook breakfast too. He was like an advert for long distance walking and good health for, with a rucksack a third the size of our own, he was wandering with no particular destination along the high ridges of the Pyrenees. "I wake up every morning and go where I want," he said with a certain indifference as he poured over his map. "That pass up there looks quite good; maybe I'll head back to France." And so he finished his breakfast, rolled everything into his sack with practised efficiency and got up. With a goodbye, he turned and bounded sprightly off on wee legs of lithe muscle. The last we saw was a small dot barrelling up a vertical scree slope a few minutes later, and then he was in France. What a remarkable man, I thought. But if such fitness and equanimity was to be ours too, then we needed to get going.

The places we stumbled across in those first few days were sublime. High, airy passes afforded long views across France and Spain while mountain tarns bound by inhospitable boulders glinted like cold steel in the sunlight. The raw beauty of the high mountains contrasted well with the water meadows below, where rivers split undecided and sauntered off through the trees. In such places long, lazy hours disappeared with the ease of summer ice-cream and we would remove our boots, pick up our books and settle under the shade of a tree. After a few days our obligations to progress began to slip. As the guidebook itinerary rushed off ahead, we hoisted two fingers to Greenwich and removed our watches. We were governed by whim and daylight now.

By the time we entered the Parc Nacional d'Aguestortes i Estany de Sant Maurici (one of Spain's most beautiful National Parks), we

knew we had reached the peak of our fitness. Our bruised hips were no longer purple; our legs were tanned and toned and our balance was finely tuned. Yet while these physical changes were predictable and expected, something completely weird happened to our senses...

We first noticed it when, wandering down a valley, we both picked up the smell of fresh soap; of washed, clean people. Now while this experience will be familiar to anyone who has spent any time without a shower, we were confused by the fact we couldn't see anyone. It wasn't until ten minutes later, when the odour was all but overpowering, that we found the picnickers responsible. And with that we realised a week and a half of fresh air had honed our sense of smell. It was the same with hearing and sight too, as the brilliant blue skies and crisp birdsong affirmed. In the absence of air pollution and the constant clamour of television, our perception had sharpened. We were turning wild again.

But there comes a point where no matter how wild and free you are, you need a bath. And, after giving up on the GR11 to wander great circles around jagged massifs, read and, for an afternoon, watch hundreds of swallows migrate south through a pass, we *really* did need a bath. So, turning around and tumbling off the hills in a bout of sheer hygienic necessity, we came to the beautiful Spanish village of Espot.

The transition from mountain to civilisation came as a shock. There was tarmac beneath our feet, cars to dodge and shops selling fresh bread. We headed straight for a bar to slake our thirst and watched childlike as the barman poured two small glasses of beer. It took just a few sips for lightheadedness to kick in, and by the time the last drop rolled out, we were plastered. But there was a shower to find and, after being welcomed by a woman clearly used to folk who have spent too long in the hills, we were installed in a room that not only had hot running water but clean sheets and a well-sprung bed. And because simple things like comfort and convenience become remarkable with very little abstinence, we giggled like simpletons at the sparkling novelty of it all. The showers we took lasted forever.

That evening, over fresh-baked trout and chips with garlic mayonnaise, we discovered that without watches or diligence we had managed to lose count of the days (it was Friday; we'd

## Fact file

### WHAT YOU NEED

We carried complete camping kit which offered freedom to stop when and where we wanted, but ended up spending as much time in bivouacs and huts as in the tent. Make sure you have a good stove (Camping Gaz and petrol are easy to find, other cartridges less so). Also be sure your boots are in good condition and fit well: 3- 4-season leather boots are best for the rough terrain. Trekking poles are also extremely useful to provide stability with a heavy pack.

Delicious... above 1500m.

### FOOD

You may have to carry up to five days' food at a time, so pack well. One reliable staple that you can buy just about anywhere is pasta and tuna with (heavy) cartons of passata. The air-dried sausages are also excellent and keep well. For breakfast, muesli or oats are a good bet, combined with powdered milk, while packet soups with noodles are an option for those with steel stomachs. Multi-vitamin pills are valuable to compensate for the potentially limited diet.

### WHEN TO GO

Summer is the most popular season in the Pyrenees, but it gets crowded and very hot. Afternoon thunderstorms are a real danger. Spring is wonderful but you may need crampons and an ice axe to negotiate lasting patches of snow, and nights will be cold. Autumn is another good bet with changeable weather and no crowds.

### ACCOMMODATION

Throughout the Pyrenees you'll find small huts and bivouacs for walkers and climbers to sleep in. Some shelters are manned and serve hot meals; others are more basic, and you'll need to cater for yourself. Most manned huts have a free bivouac section open all year, sometimes with a fireplace and often with bunks.

### GETTING THERE

Low cost airlines offer daily flights to Barcelona from the UK. From Barcelona, buses run regularly to many points in the eastern Pyrenees, for plenty of choice on where to start your route.

thought it was Wednesday). It was time to fly home at last. Two weeks in the wilderness was just enough – nature had begun to seem mundane. We had visited another world for a fortnight and come back inspired, our bodies repaired and with the most incredible feeling of lasting relaxation. And now everything, from toilets and running water to mobile phones and fridges, seemed fresh and remarkable. To say nothing of travelling in a car. So when we landed back in the UK and told long, tall tales to our friends, it was with a new energy, excitement and heightened sense of awareness. For their part, they thought we were on drugs.

It took a whole month for the effect to wear off. But although work and commuting dulls the spirit and civilisation trundles along with a certain banality, the memories are still there. I've carried with me a lasting sense of comfort that comes with knowing that those same mountains will always be there – vast and permanent – as an antidote to our crazy human existence.

As for the new-found Wilderness Man lurking inside me, well, he's resting right now, stroking his beard, picking wax from his ears and having a hearty chuckle everytime I get stressed out. Because he knows full well that his time will come again.

# ALPS THE EASY WAY

THE ALPS AREN'T ALL 'GLACIERS AND FROSTBITE'.
THERE ARE SOME VERY ACCESSIBLE SUMMITS OUT THERE,
BUT HOW COME SO FEW BRITS KNOW ABOUT THEM?

Words **Ben Winston**  Photography **Tom Bailey**

Crampons? Nope.
Rope? Nope.
Alpine summit? You betcha.

There are two schools of thought among people who avoid the Alps. There are those who've never been and reckon: "The Alps are dangerous – full of glaciers and impossible rock faces, crevasses, rock falls and avalanches. I need to know so much more before I can even dream of climbing those huge mountains."

Then there are those who've only visited the most popular locations: "The Alps? Yeah, I've been there. Great landscape, but the crowds! I've spent ages queueing to get down ladders and more sleepless nights in crowded huts than I care to remember."

In a way, both of them are right: the Alps are full of imposing mountains and crowded trails. But that's far from the whole story. Scattered all across the Alpine countries, beneath the glaciers and above the coaches and cuckoo clock villages, are hundreds – and I mean hundreds – of stunning, accessible mountains. There are so many of them that you won't know what's hit you. It's like

discovering a new Scotland, only bigger. With views of the Matterhorn and Mont Blanc. But with even just a little hill-walking experience you can find yourself, if not a high-altitude mountaineer, then at least a few thousand feet closer to being one. It's amazing – all you need to do is get on a plane (cheap), find yourself a village base (easy) and start walking. Here, follow me...

Geneva is the epitome of Swiss efficiency: land, collect luggage, pick up car, depart. But the efficiency lingers, albeit caused by the late hour and a need for rest: drive over border, arrive at Morzine, find apartment, sleep. Next morning there's something in the way the air smells that says 'Long Way From Home', though because the transition has been so swift there are moments when we're not quite sure if this is travel-lag or just the cobwebs of dreams. But the thick coffee on the hob dissolves all doubt: it's the scent of holidays.

Morzine is a crazy mix of ski chic and mountain bike absurdity: summer and winter excuses for hurtling down hills and exploring

that fine, wobbling line between virtuosity and wipe-out. This morning as we walk – a curious pastime in adrenaline's Eden – the sky is filled with colourful kites. No, not kites, but paragliders cruising thermals above. Which is where we're going: right up Pointe de Resachaux, a mountain so close and so steep it seems to rise straight out of the town's fountain. Just how I like my peaks – accessible. So with Camembert and baguettes and more Milka than you could shake a cowbell at, we enter a lush, green, flower-filled cliché: the alpine meadow. This is followed by the alpine wood: a dark, dank place where mushrooms sprout, wood rots and the smell of things growing lingers in the air. But best of all, it keeps us sheltered from the sun which, if combined with this unholiest of Alpine inclines, would squash our ambition flatter than Holland.

The hill goes on as hills do in south-eastern France, but so does the forest. It feels like a long time before the woodland gives out, the angle relents from 55 degrees for the first time in over an hour,

and France begins to appear far below. Across the treetops we discover we've stumbled into a true wonderland of peaks, all green and grassy and inviting in a strangely British way. Some have cable cars to their summits, others are simply untouched. It's odd – I expect to see path scars and tiny, stick-men silhouettes moving slowly along skylines. But there's nothing of the sort. We are alone in heaven; the entire massif is empty.

We weave up through the pasture which is dotted with shepherds' huts. Only there are no animals and no shepherds and, as we later discover, there haven't been since the locals got rich and decided to buy up the huts as summer refuges. On holidays and weekends whole families troop up here, fling open their doors and tuck into the stash of goodies that was left in spring. And how did it get here? Helicopter. Because when the snows melt and le picnic season takes hold, families group together and hire a chopper to fly up all those luxuries the British hill-walker would consider

And not a Von Trapp in sight.

unnecessary, foolish or plain cheating. So out comes the vin rouge, fizz goes the beer and, lo and behold, here comes a mountain of air-dried sausage. It's an entirely different approach, but with a glut of hills and a reliably sunny summer, perhaps it's easier to take mountains for granted, to use them as the British use parks or meadows.

Further up and it comes as a great surprise to find the summit has shed all pretence of gentle mountain and sheers off in a great cliff to the north-east. It's become a ridge; not quite knife-edge but sharp enough to give the brain a tingle. What really slams home the fact that this is the Alps is the view: Mont Blanc and the Chamonix Aiguilles; the lesser but still formidable ranges of Les Hauts Forts and, over to the north, Lake Geneva, which we can just see through a gap in the mountains. The sun is shining but it's cold at 2000m and we're having a little trouble catching our breath. So we sit down out of the breeze and try to believe what our eyes are telling us. There is enough exploring here to last a lifetime.

Day two and we hit jackpot. Fifteen minutes from Morzine and we've discovered another super-hill. It's called le Roc d'Enfer and we're being shown around by Gareth and Sam Jefferies, two Brits who gave up city life to guide mountain bikers and walkers to the local hot spots. Not an easy job, sorting the crème from the crème, but le Roc, according to Gareth, is like the better parts of the Cuillin Ridge. "It's one of the best hills in the area," he says. But I already know there are many 'best hills' around here…

It all starts benignly, up through typical meadows where the air is filled with the whistles of marmots. These weird little creatures – half cute furball, half rodent – are a favourite snack for eagles, and they know it. They scan the skies for dark shapes, finding nothing but a couple of kestrels wheeling on the thermals. But our path

leads on from the subtle drama of the natural world to a ridge. It's an approach to le Roc that can be measured in heartbeats: a steady thumpety-thump increase although the incline has levelled off.

Drops to either side are growing. By the time we're on the flank of the mountain itself our path has turned into a polished limestone scramble. It leads up through engrossing moves to a col that isn't really a col at all, but a razorblade we're somehow expected to stand on. Only this razor runs on to the north-east in a series of cuts and slashes, climbing and falling its serrated way. Credit where credit's due, this is a handsome and very fine mountain, but it's not the mountain's aesthetic appeal that has caught my attention. It's the drop. I notice it when Tom wants to take some photographs: "Stand up, look like you're enjoying yourself." I do as he says, and enjoyment seems a curious way of describing the experience. Or maybe it's not; I can't really be sure because my heart is racing and I'm longing for four points of contact. Yet slowly evolution comes with a crouch, a stoop and, finally, a two-legged standing position, although my arms still hang like a Neanderthal's. It's an unnerving feeling because here, on this grass-green spine, there is nothing to hold on to. It's like Crib Goch, only the ridge has a purer line of purpose and looks more chiselled. And on Crib Goch there are other people to follow who look more scared than you. Here, we're the only people on the hill and there is nothing but past experience to measure ability against. And with Gareth and Sam wandering nonchalantly along, it's the least we can do to stand up and follow.

Then all of a sudden something totally unexpected happens. There's a humming noise, a deep swoosh, and out of nowhere a glider soars over a ridge right there in front of us. In a wide sweep

Above: Walking the fine line between heaven and l'Enfer.
Above left: Le scrambling, c'est magnifique, n'est-ce pas?

he circles our little mountain, waving, so close we can see the dandruff in his hair. He swirls around and around, playing on le Roc's thermals. Then, when he's high enough, he peels silently away to cruise the Haute Savoie. It's a magical moment and I trace his flight over the hills. Not for the first time do I have trouble coping with the variety of the view. I want to stay forever.

On the summit it's all wild delight and satisfaction. Just over there is Mont Blanc, again. Almighty, but not as captivating to us as the hundreds of lower peaks rising into the cool air. Sam and Gareth's arms are out, waving over the landscape like wands, picking out magic hills and reciting a long French poem of seduction: Les Dents Blanches, Les Hauts Forts, Pointe de Chesery, Cornettes de Bise, Dent d'Oche… There's a lifetime of entertainment here and none of it involves ropes, axes or crampons. Or queueing. In fact, the mountains around Morzine are so perfectly suited to the British hill-walker searching new challenges, they should be covered in fog.

Which makes me wonder why they are not more popular. If this were Britain, peaks like le Roc d'Enfer would be all-time classics. People would talk about them endlessly in pubs. But the fact is that France and Switzerland and every other Alpine country simply have too much in the way of top hills; and, as a result, walkers tend to concentrate on the biggest, the hardest and, they will claim, the best. So while the Chamonix Aiguilles are heaving and Mont Blanc has a massive queue for the summit, here, just a few miles away, sits a veritable wonderland of peaks. It's the 'fame shadow' effect, and it means those of us with a British appreciation of mountains will find some of the best overlooked peaks in the world.

## Fact file

### GETTING THERE
Flights to Geneva are easy to come by and cheap these days. Fly midweek for the best fares. EasyJet flies from Luton and Liverpool – www.easyjet.com – tel. 0870 600 0000. From Geneva it's best to hire a car to let you get to the mountains – try Europcar: www.europcar.com – tel. 0845 722 2525.

### ACCOMMODATION
We stayed in one of two comfortable apartments right in the centre of Morzine. They sleep six to eight people, and can be rented from:
Alps2Go – tel. (01908) 585548; e-mail info@alps2go.com
Trek2XS – tel. (07796) 26 88 47.

### USEFUL CONTACTS
Sam and Gareth Jefferies run a walking and mountain biking company in Morzine. They can recommend walks or holidays – tel. (01202) 697448. Also check their biking website at www.endlessride.com

### TOURIST INFORMATION
Morzine TIC (00 33 4) 5074 7272; e-mail – touristoffice@morzine-avoriaz.com

### MAPS
The French IGN maps are excellent. Morzine 3528 ET (1:25,000) and the Samoens 3530 ET (1:25,000) are the most useful. Try Stanfords at www.stanfords.co.uk – tel. (020) 7434 4744 or Mapshop – tel. (01684) 593146; or buy them when you get there.

### INSURANCE
Being choppered off the hill is not a cheap experience on the continent, so it pays to take out travel insurance. The BMC arranges specialist cover for mountaineers and walkers (we used the SunSki & Climb policy) – tel. 0870 010 4878; www.thebmc.co.uk

Climbing a high mountain: just one of the many excellent things you can do in Italy's Trentino Alps.

# MULTI-ACTIVITY MELTDOWN

A SKI RESORT WITH NO SNOW SOUNDS DISTINCTLY UNPROMISING. BUT, AS TOM HUTTON DISCOVERED, IT MADE THE PERFECT BASE FOR A SUMMER ADVENTURE.

Photography **Tom Hutton**

**P**acking has never been my strong point. I always leave it to the last minute and end up cobbling together a selection of kit that, at best, will do the job. Saying that, I've never found myself short of anything vital; and anyway, trying to work out what I've forgotten gives me something to do on the flight.

This trip would be different, though; if we were to maximise our chances of real adventure we would need to plan our kit list with military precision. Bike shoes, shorts, helmets, even pedals! Walking boots, climbing helmets, crampons, ropes... It read like a stock-take for Snow+Rock, and trying to cram it all into just two rucksacks was a bit like a qualifier for *The Krypton Factor*. We passed the first hurdle though and, as the plane touched down at Venice airport that sunny, late-summer morning, we were filled with a sudden rush of genuine excitement, the kind you get when you wake up and remember it's your birthday: you have absolutely no idea what's in store for you but you know it's gonna be good.

Our mission was simple – multi-activity with a capital M. Hike, bike, climb, raft, kayak – anything as long as it involved adrenaline. It felt like a recycling scheme on a grand scale: take the leftovers from the multi-billion pound ski industry and convert them into affordable, achievable and enjoyable mountain adventures for all. Lift systems provide a quick and easy way out of the valleys; ski-pistes often make excellent mountain bike trails; hotels that normally thrive on budding Franz Klammers make inexpensive valley bases; and even rafting utilises a by-product of the winter wonderland itself – melting snow.

Our tiny hire car's suspension sagged as we threw our bags into the back. It was late afternoon when we reached Folgaría, a bustling Alpine village in the foothills of the Dolomites which, we had on good authority, would make a great base for some of the best local mountain bike trails. The surrounding mountains were a daunting prospect for a pair of unacclimatised cyclists, but we needn't have worried: we had a lift system to help us out.

Now, taking a bike on a lift was a strange concept. My companion Steph and I are both from the 'old school' of riders who believe that you haven't earned the descent until you've conquered the climb; but this, as was quickly pointed out by JP from Folgaría Trentino Bike Tours, missed the point completely. Apparently it's not about making it easy for yourself; the lifts simply allow you to go further and see more using the same effort. Put this way, we wondered why it hadn't caught on in the Dales! We duly collected our two full-suspension bikes and bundled them into a rusty-looking lift.

The view from the top, deserved or not, was simply breath-taking. The Brenta Dolomites, sporting a bright coating of fresh snow, dominated the skyline, and all we could hear was the sound of cow bells tinkling in the valley below. We pushed the last few metres to the summit, heaved ourselves into the saddle, and prepared for the first of many mouth-watering descents. The track started off easily enough, but it soon required all our skill and attention just to stay upright. Steph was the first to taste Italian dirt; and though she came up smiling, she did point out that it could do with a spot more black pepper and some parmesan to be really enjoyable. What followed was a couple of hours of wide gravel tracks, grassy hillsides and kilometre after kilometre of steep and technical singletrack; all with lifts at the bottom to carry us swiftly back up. We covered many miles, but recovered quickly enough to enjoy some Italian-style après-bike before retiring for the day – with more of the same planned for tomorrow.

From Folgaría, we drove 2 hours north, to the village of Dimaro. This was to be the start of a trip down the formidable River Noce, involving 28km of navigable snowmelt with very cold water and rapids up to Grade V. A tall order in a kayak, for sure; but in a fully inflated raft with a guide at the helm, *no problemo*! With the sun shining and the water clear and blue, the ride proved to be fantastic: a continuous flow of fast-moving white water, with plenty of rocks to avoid and countless holes and waves to get munched in. Although it was quite late in the season and the water levels were starting to drop off, by the end of the descent we were both exhausted but happy and very, very wet.

Later on we took stock – over a glass of Chianti, of course. We'd cycled the foothills, slept in the villages, eaten in the restaurants, drunk in the bars and even got drenched in the rivers, but now it was time for the main course: the mountains themselves. Italy is justly famous for the imposing limestone towers of the Dolomites; however, there are plenty of other high peaks to pit your skills and stamina against. From Malè, it's a short drive to Peio Fonti – a cable car station nestled at the foot of the impressive Ortles-Cevedale mountain range. We intended to climb to a refuge that night then make a traverse of the main ridge tomorrow. It was a big plan but, by using lifts, we were able to cut out the first 908m of the climb. And before anyone accuses us of cheating, I should point out that there was a further 1200m to climb on foot – and that was just to the refuge!

Due to the glaciated nature of the terrain and the tough-looking conditions, we'd hired an Alpine guide, Stefano, who led us off at a steady pace on a steep and narrow path that wound its way up the mountain. We climbed in silence, stopping only for the occasional drink and to admire the view that was unfolding behind us. Cloud obscured the summit, but the path was technical enough to demand our concentration. We crossed the snowline at around 2800m, which was low for the time of year. Indeed, it seemed that winter was due to arrive early in Trentino; and, only a few minutes later, it started to rain. Our troubles didn't end there. The wind, which had been ever-present since the top of the last lift, had now developed into something approaching storm force; and, as we climbed yet higher, the rain turned to snow making us grateful for the guiding hand ropes that guarded the trickier sections. We focused on following Stefano and occupied our minds by counting the red paint splashes on the rock that marked the way.

"Half way!" came a faint voice above the howl of the wind. We looked up to see Stefano a few metres ahead, hardly breathing; he looked fitter than the two of us put together. We took another quick drink and used the opportunity to add an extra layer in an attempt to insulate ourselves from what were rapidly becoming full-on

"...the ride was fantastic: a continuous flow of fast-moving white water, with plenty of rocks to avoid and countless holes and waves to get munched in..."

On the River Noce, where inflation is a good thing.

Aftermath of sudden summer snowstorm, descending Vioz.

conditions we frequently stumbled into deep snowdrifts. Forty five minutes later, we posed briefly for that all-important summit shot and lamented the lack of a view that should have included the impressive Forni glacier and the infamous '13 Peaks'.

On the descent there was no sign of our earlier tracks; it felt like a whole new route. We made steady progress back to the hut, carefully threading the rope around pinnacles as we went. There was no way we could complete the planned route in these conditions, so we resigned ourselves to a long walk back down the path we'd fought so hard to climb the previous day.

Typically, no sooner had we left the hut than the cloud dispersed and we were bathed in brilliant sunshine. We consoled ourselves with the breathtaking views: glistening white powder covered the slopes and, for the first time, we were gazing out over typical high mountain scenery. We dropped beneath the snowline and were soon striding confidently over the lush green meadows of the valley floor. It was hard to take our eyes away from Vioz, which by now was a pristine white pyramid against a clear blue sky. The ridge traverse was not to be ours this time; but we did, at least, have the summit climb to remember the trip by.

According to Stefano, there's a myth in these parts about a strongbox full of treasure. It was supposed to have been buried in a castle long ago to conceal it from advancing Venetian troops and, despite concerted digging many years later, it had never been found. After a week of adrenaline-pumped activity, we heaved our aching limbs into our trusty little car and set off for the airport knowing that we'd discovered some hidden treasure of our own – summer in Trentino, a multi-activity paradise.

winter conditions. The views would have been spectacular but we were now thoroughly immersed in a thick blanket of cloud. Higher and higher we trudged, buffeted by the full force of the storm. Suddenly, through a brief window in the cloud, we caught sight of the hut. The Mantova Al Vioz, at 3535m the highest refuge in the Central and Western Alps, was just a few metres ahead. We burst through the door and were greeted by a powerful blast of steamy warm air and the wonderful aroma of fresh pasta. We ate a well-deserved dinner and retired early; tomorrow would be a big day.

There's an age-old dilemma in the mountains. In good conditions, you set off long before dawn and get the day over with early; but when things are less than perfect, you have a big decision to make. Wait it out to see if it improves – possibly at the expense of the time need to complete your trip. Alternatively, head out anyway and pray that it improves – at least enough for you to enjoy yourself safely. Sadly, Sod's first law of mountain travel states that whichever you choose will be the wrong one, and we were granted no exemptions the next morning. We waited and waited before finally deciding to cut the itinerary short, make an out-and-back summit dash onto Monte Vioz itself, and then enjoy a leisurely descent to the security of the valley.

Things hadn't improved one iota as we wrestled our way out of the hut and donned our crampons in the entrance lobby. The wind was swirling around us in relentless blasts and the snow was being driven hard into our stinging faces. We roped up and, with Stefano once more in the lead, set out into the weather.

On a good day, it's only a 15 minute walk from the Mantova refuge to the impressive 3645m summit of Monte Vioz. This was not a good day. We struggled upwards at a painfully slow place, our faces now numb from the freezing wind and flying snow, stopping frequently to brace ourselves against particularly forceful gusts that threatened to topple us from the ridge. Our crampons scraped regularly over bare rock and in the near white-out

# Fact file

## GETTING THERE
We flew Stansted to Venice Marco Polo Airport with Go – tel. (0870) 607 6543 www.go-fly.com Other options for Trentino include Ryanair to Verona and Treviso – tel. (0870) 333 1231 (www.ryanair.com). For maximum freedom (essential for multi-activity breaks), hire a car, via either of the airlines or most of the major international operators (www.hertz.com; www.budget.com; www.goalamo.com)

## ACCOMMODATION
Folgaría – Club Hotel Alpino – tel. (00 39) 464 721102 e-mail; hotelalpino@tin.it – a nice hotel with a mountain bike rental shop and guiding service attached. They also offer mountain bike and multi-activity holiday packages. Malè – La Segosta Lodge – tel. (00 39) 463 901390, (www.segosta.com) which had nice rooms and an excellent restaurant. The refuges can be booked via the tourist board.
There's stacks of accommodation choices for all budgets in both areas; for further information contact the Trentino Infoservice – tel. (020) 8879 1405 (www.trentino.to)

## WHAT TO TAKE
We took equipment for just about every activity we could think of as well as shorts and T-shirts for those sunny rest days! Choose from full winter walking gear, mountain bike wear, helmets and climbing rack. You can hire crampons, ice axes and climbing gear; a guide may even be able to supply them. Wetsuits are supplied by rafting companies and quality bikes can also be hired locally (we got ours from Club Hotel Alpino in Folgaría).

## WHEN TO GO
Generally, in resorts, the lifts re-open for summer in June and close again in September. Check first with the tourist office if you're relying on these for your adventures. Weather-wise, the climate in most of the Alps is quite kind from spring through autumn; but be prepared for storms in the afternoons and wintry conditions at altitude.

## BOOKS AND MAPS
Good quality maps for almost all of the Alps are normally available from local tourist offices, or in the UK try Stanfords (www.stanfords. co.uk). Walking in the Alps by Kev Reynolds or Summits for All: The French Alps – 100 Easy Mountains for Walkers by Edouard Prevoste and Jill Neate both give a taste for what's on offer if you're on foot. In general, tourist boards and local offices can provide details of activities available in their area.

## OTHER USEFUL CONTACTS
Rafting centre, Dimaro – tel. (00 39) 463 973278; www.raftingcenter.it
Val di Sole Alpine guides, Malè – tel. (00 39) 463 901151; or contact via tourist board.

Chata pri Zelenom hut.
Located somewhere near Eden.

# MENTAL BLOC

### THERE'S NOTHING BORDERLINE ABOUT THE TATRA MOUNTAINS, AS **BEN WINSTON** FOUND ON A MEMORABLE TRIP OUT EAST...

One foot in Poland, the other in Slovakia; standing high on a ridge that marks an international border should be an amazing feeling. It should be one of those moments where whooping, screaming and waving your arms at the view is an understated and rational reaction. But it wasn't. The cloud was thick and I was too busy entertaining notions of death to consider singing the Tatras' praises. We were on the Eagle's Path (the 'eagle' part is descriptive, the 'path' bit simply inaccurate) and all I could focus on was the unique potential of falling to my death in one of two different countries.

Off to my left was a burial in Zakopane where I could share the earth with some of Poland's finest mountaineers. To my right, the express route to the symbolic cemetery, a beautiful little garden of placards and crosses remembering Slovakia's greatest outdoor heroes. But whichever way I went there was some solace to be had in the fact I could be sure my body would be found – the Tatra mountain rescue teams on both sides of the border are known as some of the best in the world.

But it isn't all as hairy as this. The Tatra are for walking and offer 600km of well-made trails by way of proof. Craggy valleys, high passes, gentle woodland, teardrop lakes, Alpine peaks and a prolific network of cheap mountain huts are just some of the reasons that regular, two-feet-on-the-ground walking is something of an institution in Poland and Slovakia. Yet there's more to it than that. At a not very long 29km and covering a not-exactly-vast 260 sq km, the High Tatra are one of the smallest high mountain ranges in the world, so they're remarkably accessible and perfect for a quick holiday, if only you could do the place justice in that time. Which you can't. Because when you add all that walking to untold amounts of via ferrata, climbing, scrambling, lightweight multi-day adventures utilising the huts, plenty of 2500m-plus summits and the chance to cross an international border on a 2499m peak, you end up with a seriously enticing trip. Which begs the question – why are we happy to pay over the odds for crowded French mountains when the Tatra, with all their variety and none of the dangers of glaciers and high altitude, are willing and waiting?

It may be because Eastern Europe suffers from our Western European preconceptions. The very term 'Eastern Bloc' conjures up notions of boiled potatoes, cabbage and vodka; dour, dumpy women serving beetroot soup and endless cities of monotonous grey housing. Well, all that is

High above the Téryho chata hut in a late season snowfield.

true, but since Poland and Slovakia (then Czechoslovakia) gave Communism the boot in 1989, this bleak, Orwellian image is a long way from the bigger picture. Because since then everyone seems to have spent a good deal of time and effort embracing capitalism. Take the southern Polish mountain town of Zakopane for instance, where, while you can still get a dill, potato and pickled cabbage meal in a grey restaurant from the ladle of a Communist mamma for the equivalent of 50p, you can also find restaurants where whole roast pigs are served, where you can buy the finest French wines and where they take Visa gold cards with a smile. You can buy Gucci there, or Armani, or fritter away your zloty on the latest in ski chic.

But despite the relentless march towards globalisation, I started my trip in a manner that was both time-honoured and thoroughly traditional: with a bunch of very friendly locals, vodka and beer. And that is why, later that evening, an incoherent westerner was seen stumbling down the high street, singing and blinking furiously at passing women in the mistaken belief that he was top dog in Zakopane. He wasn't, and he learned two important lessons. The first is that locals can always drink more than you can. The second is that downing heinous quantities of the local spirit does not make you fluent in Polish.

The following morning, Kasparowy Wierch (a huge local mountain) and a particularly pernicious weather front had divided my group into three camps. There were optimists ("Don't worry, it'll be clear on top"), pessimists ("This is as bad as Britain") and those of us too ill to offer an opinion. As it turned out both the conjectures were wrong; the first because hope and prayers cannot clear cumulus, and the second because there is nowhere in the UK where you can get into a Communist era cable car and ascend to 1985m. But I couldn't help but think how perfectly academic all of this was, because in only a few hours I could be dead from either vodka poisoning or a hangover stumble. But we were already committed. We clambered into the cable car and juddered up to the summit to join the crowds of Poles, all of whom seemed to be wearing day-glo pac-a-macs. In contrast to these offensively bright garments, most wore expressions of grey and stared deep into the fug with a look that was an act of either deep philosophy or simple resignation. Then we were joined by our guide – a man dressed in corduroys and chequered shirt and who greeted us with a hearty "Velcome" – and led off into the cloud.

The Eagle's Path started as a gentle affair along a baby whaleback. It continued innocuously enough until we rounded on the 2301m Swinica, where things began to go a little pear-shaped. Here, our guide explained, many people die each year from lightning strikes. The record is nine dead in one lightning-bolt slaughterfest – think final scene of *Raiders of the Lost Ark* and you'll get the picture. And after Swinica, things got worse. Within the space of 20 minutes the path had turned into a tenuous thread of chains across rock slabs, and the lowlands of both Poland and Slovakia seemed significantly quicker to get to. However, an hour later the hangover had become a hang-on-or-die-er, and I began to enjoy myself. The lack of views was a little disappointing but the scrambling was of such quality, the rock architecture so dramatic, that with the natural resignation of an Englishman it wasn't too hard to be happy. Especially when we finally descended to find that in Poland, mountain huts exist primarily to serve food and beer in huge quantities.

By the time I made it to Slovakia a few days later things had calmed down. My group of heavy-drinking companions had departed and I had been joined by a far more sober childhood friend. So we crossed the border into Poland's poor neighbour and immediately set about getting to grips with the country that hosts four-fifths of the High Tatra. It didn't take long. In spite of a vocabulary that extended no further than pivo (beer) and vodka (vodka), we found our way from Tatranská Kotlina up into the mountains. They were limestone at first and sported some enormous cliffs, but our route led along ridges that were perfectly balanced between knife-edge fear and whaleback security. Till we reached a lake like a mirror in which the Tatra hung disconcertingly upside down, and where life took a turn for the leisurely as we followed the path around to a five star location hotel. Nestled above a lake at the end of a valley straight out of a fairytale, Chata pri Zelenom was a hut without precedent. In fact, it wasn't a hut. It was Eden.

Next morning dawned bright and early, and we set off for a steep climb out of the valley. Skirting beneath the huge tumbledown cliffs of Lomnicky stít, we climbed an improbable path higher and higher until, at the top and not far from fainting with exertion, we pulled over the ridge to find Slovakia stretched out below. It was stunning; but of far more immediate concern was a towering storm cloud just before us, a huge pillar of

High and exposed in Slovakia – storm clouds brewing behind.

The only way is down.

# COVERING A NOT-EXACTLY-VAST 260 SQ KM, THE HIGH TATRA ARE ONE OF THE SMALLEST HIGH MOUNTAIN RANGES IN THE WORLD, SO THEY'RE REMARKABLY ACCESSIBLE AND PERFECT FOR A QUICK HOLIDAY

past with a cheery 'good day', untroubled by their sweaty plastic ponchos and their carrier bags full of lunch, and bolted on up the hill, over the 2000m contour, past the hut and over the pass. We stood dumbfounded, but continued our descent regardless.

So by the time we had new boots and were attempting to get back into Poland via Rysy, a 2499m peak and the only place you can legally cross the international border in the mountains, we weren't too surprised to find ourselves following two bright orange pac-a-macs through a blizzard. The going wasn't easy with ice forming on the path and snow blowing into every chink in the armour of our jackets, so we could only imagine how the pair up front were doing. But they didn't seem to care, and stormed on over the rocks, pulling at the sections of frozen chains without gloves, flat-footing their Doc Marten-style boots on the névé and trundling right on over the summit, oblivious to the clearing weather and the finest views of the week. Mid-June in the Tatra and all I could see was a winter landscape of ragged peaks and haunting blue tarns; ridges squiggling off in every direction, a sea of tantalising unclimbed (by me) peaks, plus two specks of orange plastic billowing somewhere below us in Poland. It was delightful to be stood there once again with one foot on either side of the border, fearlessly now, happy at being graced with the view yet wondering why the mountains had waited right to the end before showing us their full, ruthless glory. But then perhaps this was deliberate. Perhaps this was a cliffhanger – the mountains' parting shot; the reason we needed to return for the next episode. With the variety of adventures laid out there before us, it was an invitation only the foolish could refuse.

But, to be honest, I'd be going back even if this trump view hadn't been played; and it's because as a good Zakopane friend of mine said on our first night: "The vodka bottle is empty. I'll buy the next."

And I still owe him one. Hic…

cumulonimbus billowing out in what geography teachers will tell you is a classic anvil shape. This cloud looked decidedly evil. Within minutes it had enveloped us, and a relentless flashing and booming began; but we couldn't see where the lightning was striking. With hair standing on end in fear, we hurtled down the path, dodging rocks and turning steeply on scree, running for all we were worth, looking hopelessly for shelter in a desolate landscape. For 15 minutes terror reigned, the words of the Polish guide and Swinica's death toll ringing in my ears; and then, just as suddenly as the cloud had wrapped us up, it released us. We were safe.

Next morning we stepped out from the 2015m Téryho chata hut full of purpose. We were going to cross the Priecne sedlo, a 2352m pass. Yet we quickly discovered that grand intentions count for naught when your boots fall apart; and as the rough granite path welcomed us again, that's exactly what happened to my walking partner's footwear. So we turned around, defeated, and descended to the valley. Only after an hour we were shamed by Slovakians – lots of them – all wearing trainers. They stormed on

# VLAD

## ONCE YOU'VE BEEN WALKING IN TRANSYLVANIA, IT'S IN

I should have take Latin classes more seriously. Actually, I should probably have taken the whole of my brief period of schooling more seriously. But Latin really lost me. "Amo, amas, a minibus." Yeah, yeah. And in just what bizarre set of circumstances, exactly, would I ever need to address a piece of furniture in the vocative voice? "*Mensa* – O table – my passions have been inflamed by the shapeliness of your rococo legs – fancy a dance?" Well, yes, perhaps.

But some knowledge of Latin, in theory anyway, would actually help in understanding modern Romanian. While a smidgen of history and geography – lessons which I passed while perfecting the ultimate in delta-wing, rubber-band-powered paper dart design – wouldn't go amiss in getting some grasp of the bizarre complexities of the country and its people. Because Romania, and particularly its central region of Transylvania, is a far-flung outpost

of ancient Latin culture, with Mediterranean passions and Italian-quality corruption. And it's even stranger for being surrounded by countries – Hungary, Russia, Bulgaria and Serbia – whose populations speak much weirder languages and have completely different histories.

How did this mix-up come about? Well, in the first century AD, the Roman Emperor Trajan, as part of his ambitions for pre-Coca-Cola-and-McDonalds globilisation, led two successful campaigns against the kingdom of the Dacians, the majority population of the area that is now Romania. Under the occupying force there was a brief period of hot baths and straight roads before the effort of subjugating the insurgent tribes got too costly and the top-brass Latins legged it back to Chiantiland. But they left a fair number of their minor officials and 'grunts', as well as large chunks of their language, behind them, in the 'land beyond the forest,' as

Above: What car? Striding out en route to Malincrav.
Left: A carved gate leading to the village church,
at Lunca Ilvei on the Transylvanian/Moldavian border.

# INFINITUM

## THE BLOOD. JASPER WINN RETURNS TO AN OLD HAUNT.

Photography **Jasper Winn**

Transylvania translates. So, Romania became something of an abandoned Italy-on-the-Black-Sea.

And there were other incomers after the Romans. Hungarian Magyars. German Saxons. Gypsies. Serbs. Ukrainians. And, for all I know, Congolese pygmies and gap-year Martians. Making Romania just about the least comprehensible country in Europe, with a richer tapestry of competing musics, odd rural customs and plain barmy folklore than you'll find anywhere outside of your own local Morris dancing club. It's also one of the most rewarding lands for walking trips.

I'd done a bit of both – misunderstanding the Romanians and taking long strolls through their country – on two visits there in the 1980s of the Cold War. I came away with memories of shepherds in ground-sweeping sheepskin cloaks, abstruse political arguments, alcohol that could twist your head right off

and relocate it somewhere down around your boots; and an awe-inspiringly dramatic landscape of deciduous forests, rolling high pastures and tight-folded valleys, all crisscrossed by paths trodden out by Romanian villagers trekking off to visit other villagers over the next hill. I rather wanted to return.

Last winter, Christina and I were invited by an Austrian friend to spend New Year in her rustic, 'getaway' house in the small Transylvanian village of Stejarisu. We'd see in 2001 amid the snows and beech forests of southern Romania. "You'll love it," Andrea told us. " There's wonderful walking. And there are wolves, too, up in the forests, though you won't actually see them." We hesitated. "And there's no television." It was the clincher. Good walking, a hint of wolf and avoiding Seven Brides for Seven Brothers, all in one trip. Irresistible.

The three of us caught the train from Vienna, a few days after

Sheep and cheerful accommodation, Transylvania-style.

Andrea and Christina, concentrating hard on navigation.

Christmas. We chugged across Hungary in the night, crossed the border and, shortly past dawn, got off in Sighisora. A rattletrap, cross-county taxi ride later and we were in Stejarisu. Andrea turned a huge, blacksmith-crafted key in the lock of her door. I was pointed towards a pile of logs and an axe under a lean-to. Christina was dispatched to the end of the garden to windlass up buckets of water from the well.

A fire was stoked up in the cast-iron kitchen stove, a kettle put on to boil, the food piled on shelves and a besom piloted across the dusty floorboards. Chores done, we were free to pull on our boots and walk. Which is what everybody else in the village was doing. The only difference being that they had to walk and we chose to.

For the villagers of Transylvania, where cars are rare and those few there are spend a good deal of their life broken down, walking is a part of life. It's what you do to gather firewood, to get to the fields and to herd sheep. It's your primary means of transport. So taking a walk isn't exactly a leisure activity, eagerly looked forward to as a break from everyday life. For most rural Romanians, putting one foot in front of the other, for hours on end, day after day, in all kinds of weather, is everyday life. But we were on holiday and so spent our days in the incomprehensible occupation, from the villagers' point of view, of walking for absolutely no purpose at all.

Each day Christina and I climbed up to the wooded hills on either side of the deep valley that cradled Stejarisu, and wandered

the ridges, or struck off into the thick beech forests or just perambulated around the frozen fields. It was dull, grey, chill weather, and any villager who wasn't out herding sheep, or striding the 4km to the nearest road to catch a lift to the nearest town, or doing something agricultural with hoe and spade, was sitting in the village bar drinking beer or huddling next to their stove. Before, invariably, having to walk home, or head outside to get firewood.

On New Year's Eve, it snowed. Sitting by the stove, sipping tzuicla – plum spirits – we heard the gate open, and a tentative shuffling on the wooden boards of the veranda. There was a knock on the door. Looking out, we saw two small boys, one with a huge whip and the other with a handbell. Nervously they launched into a sing-song blessing of both the house and us. Then, suddenly brave, they rounded on the malevolent beings that, in the land of Dracula, forest goblins, evil dictators and wolves, are always assumed to be hanging around in the darkness ready to cause mischief.

Cracking the whip in great whirling explosions, and ringing the bell like a machine-gun, they drove out the bad of the past year and welcomed in the good spirits and fine weather. We gave them chocolate and oranges. All the while the snow tumbled down on their heads, and piled up around their boots.

The snow fell through the night, and when we woke at dawn

The horse's red plume is to ward off the evil eye.

Sleepy Stejarisu, 'Best Christmas Card Cover' winner 100 years on the trot.

Tired of walking? Try this! In the hills above Lunca Ilvei.

the next day, the village and the surrounding fields and hills had been reprinted as a high-contrast, black and white photograph. We had planned to walk the 12km over the high, northern hills to the village of Malincrav, have a drink and then walk back by the same route. The 'route' was a faint track, now under a thickish covering of snow. We decided to go anyway.

Patches of blue were wedging the snow clouds further and further apart as we stomped off through the village, boots crunching the crisp snow as if we were walking on crumpled tinfoil. Children were scooting down the fields on sledges, and groups of villagers were stepping out along every compass bearing to cross the surrounding hills to visit other villages. After a few kilometres we turned off the cart track and climbed up into the hills. A hare spurted out from under a snow-domed bush, throwing up little explosions of ice from under its feet like cartoon speed puffs. Between the wide-spaced trees, fox, stoat and crow prints in the snow showed where the local fauna had hunted and scavenged. Just as, looking back, our own footprints indicated our stop-start, zigzag progress up the slopes. We may have persuaded ourselves away from the warm stove with the aim of actually reaching somewhere; but as the sun rose higher and the colours grew ever more intense ,we began strolling rather than walking. We were easily distracted by the urgent need for snowball fights. And for sips from my hip flask. We talked more and walked less.

Up on the ridge the trees opened out, giving a clear view to the Fagaras Mountains forming a hazy horizon far, far to the west of the forests and fields beneath us. We didn't talk at all, then, and walked even slower. There was the distant 'plunking' of an axe falling again and again into hard, sap-drained wood. Closer there were piles of fire lumber waiting to be collected by horsedrawn sleighs when the snow was deeper. We tramped on, stamping our feet against the cold.

"Malincrav is in the valley over there, just below the trees." We had reached the end of the ridge and were looking down into dark woods. Andrea was pointing. " We're about halfway there, so it'll take another hour and a half to reach it." But we'd rather lost interest in going to the village. Or, even, in getting to the bar. Like the Romanian children, we were on holiday, freed from all ideas of actually achieving anything.

Two young men came over the hilltop towards us. Andrea recognised them. "They're from Malincrav, but they have family in Stejarisu." They carried a half-full (or, more correctly, half-empty) bottle of tzuicla, and were stopping every few hundred metres to uncork it, take a swig and then stand talking, with exaggerated gestures, before walking on. They weren't marching with any more purpose than us. They passed across the bottle when we met, and

we sucked in burning mouthfuls, spluttering "Noroc!" – cheers – with each draught. From where we were standing they could have cut across the hills and taken the direct route to Stejarisu, but instead they chose to stride off down the long, looping, logging road, polka-dotted with horse hoofprints, that skirted the woods. It was a longer but prettier route. Nobody, it seemed, was in a hurry to get anywhere.

Not even the old couple we met when we finally turned back towards home in the falling sun of the late afternoon. "Lydia's mother and father…they'll be going to Malincrav to see their family," announced Andrea when they were close enough for her to recognise them, referring to a girl we had met the previous day. She called out loud greetings: "*Buna seara! Ce mai faceti?*" It certainly sounded Latin, or at least Italian.

The man and the woman eased their bundles and stopped to chat. "What wonderful weather, and how good the track is. Isn't it a joy to be alive and walking today?" they exclaimed in Romanian. They seemed unhurried on their journey. "We'll get there just before dark," they reckoned, "or a bit later."

On this New Year's Day, under a blue sky, with the dropping sun lighting up the crystalline snow and turning the fallen leaves under the beeches into glowing embers, walking was suddenly fun. Even for the villagers. People who normally walked because they had to were out walking for pleasure. We began to feel less of an oddity.

Entering the woods, we backtracked along Lydia's parents' footprints, following a twisting track between the soaring, dull-silver columns of the tree trunks for another hour. A buzzard mewed overhead but out of sight. By dusk we were looking down on Stejarisu again. Coils of smoke twirled up from the chimneys, faintly tanging the air. Distant figures, like Lowry stick-men, moved around their yards or brought horses in from the fields. There was the muffled barking of a dog. Two shepherds were driving a flock of sheep past the houses with shrill whistles and snatches of song. As they passed the gate to each yard a couple or trio of sheep would peel off, like returning commuters, and trot into their own stalls.

We paused among the trees before plunging down the slope towards the house, heat and supper. It had been a perfect day of gloriously pointless walking. Suddenly I realised what the vocative case was all about. Maybe I'd never need to ask a table to dance, or not without drinking a lot more tzuicla at any rate, but now I addressed the landscape, mouthing the words silently: "O sun! O snow! O hills! O trees!" Then I thought for a few moments and added: "O roaring fire! O sausage! O glass of *tzuicla!*"

# SIERRA NIRVANA

DONE ALL THE USUAL UK THINGS? WANT A NEW STORY TO TELL? THEN YOU NEED TO WIDEN YOUR HORIZONS, HOP ON A PLANE AND HAVE YOURSELF AN ADVENTURE.

Words and photography **Ben Winston**

So you've done the Three Peaks. You've completed the Welsh 3000ers. You've even raised £200 for Auntie McSpringle's Black Toenail Appeal by ticking off a well-known long distance path. But not long after you get back, you wake up in your normal bed in your normal house with your normal work to return to, and have to face the inevitable question: 'Whatever will I do next?'

You need a new challenge, something to push your limits and make for a good tale down the pub. Well, there are the Munros, but they involve years of dedication. There's Mont Blanc, but that requires money, time and experience you don't yet have. You don't fancy an adventure race and don't particularly feel like repeating the Three Peaks on one leg, so what are you going to do?

High on the summit of Mulhacén, Spain laid out beneath.

The answer is to find a trip that strikes a balance between accessible adventure and worthwhile challenge. It needs to be daring enough to earn your mates' respect and accessible enough to be undertaken while holding down a job. It shouldn't leave your credit card smouldering, needs to be achievable in a week and can't be something everyone you know has already done.

So how about a winter ascent of Spain's highest peak?

At 3482m, Mulhacén is a bold confirmation that Spain has big mountains other than those of the Pyrenees. It sits unexpectedly south of the best part of everywhere, poking above the city of Granada and not too far from the time-share fest that is the Costa Del Sol. And while it may be almost 3500m, there are no glaciers to fall into or acclimatisation to deal with. You can climb it with Scottish winter skills, some warm, sturdy kit and a wee bit of luck. Best of all, at just a few hours from most British airports, it is a mountain of instant adventure. It's perfect for Pot Noodle fame: that just-add-water glory.

So in one of my periodic attempts to become the nonchalant mountaineer ('Just popping over to climb Spain's highest mainland peak. Back on Wednesday – don't cancel the milk'), I found myself on an overcrowded charter plane cruising south.

In Malaga I found my friend Astri, we got swiftly onto a bus and were soon speeding towards the village of Trevélez, high in the Alpujarras: the foothills of the Sierra Nevada. It's one of those places where life moves at half speed, dogs bark in slow motion, everything revolves around slow, repetitive conversations, and days are lost as easily as loose change.

We stocked up with three days' supplies and found an old man with huge, callused hands to show us the start of the track. He walked us to the last house and pointed up a hill and away into a valley, saying something like "*Es imposible, amigos*" before turning back, shaking his head and muttering "Loco, loco, loco" as if climbing Mulhacén in winter was the maddest thing he'd ever heard of.

**THE ALHAMBRA**
Sometimes called one of the Wonders of the World, the Alhambra palace and its gardens are the 'must see's of nearby Granada. From them you can see Mulhacén.

By the time the sun went down we had made little progress into the hills, but just enough to escape the sloth of Trevélez. We found a little spur jutting out into the main valley that provided no shelter but a reasonably flat bed, then set up camp. Our gear spread out into a wide circle around us: four-season sleeping bags, down jackets, pile jackets, thick hats, spare gloves, fleece salopettes, thermal undies, axes, crampons, and the sort of solid tent you can roll elephants over and still get a good night's kip in. As the temperature plummeted and the distant snows swapped their pink for a frigid electric blue, I gave thanks to my mother's insistence on packing a few more warmth-enhancing layers. We lit a fire from a few sparse twigs and mounds of dried cow dung, then settled back to watch the stars spread out in the sky above. The last of the cattle bells eventually stopped clanging and then, apart from the crackle of the fire, it was silent. The Milky Way seared through the night.

The next morning we sniffed out the Dog's Arse River Valley, or Vallee de Rio Culo de Pero, as the locals call it. The name perfectly describes how a walker feels following a day struggling up through its tangled, spiky scrub, an overweight rucksack bruising shoulders and hips, dust mingling with sweat to form a thick cake of mud. But the valley quickly improved as we gained height – the ground hardening and snow patches appearing, then the river froze spectacularly as it fell through a series of boulders, reduced to a hollow tinkling from somewhere behind the blue pipes.

It wasn't until we pulled over the lip of La Cañada de Siete

Lagunas, however, that things turned truly spectacular. Roughly translated as The Valley of the Seven Lakes, it was a beautiful amphitheatre of frozen lagoons and the vast, ice-encrusted faces of Mulhacén and Alcazaba: a startling place to camp. With the sun beginning to set and the temperature plummeting wildly, we ignored the scenery and scrabbled for a piece of ground on which to put up the tent, using clusters of rocks for the guys since the frozen earth wasn't in the mood for pegs. As we worked I watched my thermometer dropping degrees by the minute – before long it was freezing, then five, then ten below. Wrapped in every available layer, we started supper, then sat back to watch the last purples and pinks fade from this high, silent and hauntingly beautiful landscape. Only when food was ready did the stars come out, several slipping on the ice and tumbling to earth. It was so peaceful, it could have been death.

Come the morning, things had changed. Shivering in spite of our layers, we woke to a shower of ice. Our breath had condensed and frozen beautifully to the tent's inner walls. We clambered out into a lazy dawn and vowed that once the sun was on us we'd begin the final push to the summit. But when the sun arrived, we couldn't muster the will to leave. Up there, high above the world and so far from anything that mattered, time began to take on the same syrupy quality that we'd seen in Trevélez, oozing, thick and sweet. So in celebration of the Andulacian clock and another fine Spanish day in the making, we pulled our roll mats into the sun, put on sunscreen and lay back to read. After an hour or so a herd of ibex came to play on the lip of the valley, completely unconcerned by English folk relaxing at 3000m, dressed in T-shirts in the depths of winter. They eventually wandered off and, at what would normally have been lunchtime, we decided we really should do the same.

As we gained height our lungs heaved and our legs turned to lead. Regular rests became mandatory. We were sluggish puppets, and the strain of hauling reluctant bodies higher and higher above Spain made us feel like proper, seasoned mountaineers attempting a serious and difficult peak. Which we weren't, of course, because now we were on the summit ridge not only could we see the road that leads to the top in summer (the easy, less spectacular way). But we were well aware that neither of us had been to this sort of height in winter before. And something was nagging me that, just possibly, it was luck that had brought us this far.

At the summit proper we collapsed into the lee of a ruin to escape the gusts whipping up the vicious north face (a sheer 500m plummet). A metal cross that once stood proud had been snapped in two by the elements and now swung from a thread of metal, clanging disconsolately in the wind. It was a haunting place, but we decided to wrap up and wait for a spectacular sunset.

When the light finally turned golden it became clear that all was not well with the weather. The wind, previously confined to the north face, had begun to gust over the tops, picking up mad dervishes of spindrift and whipping them into frenzies. They danced like ghosts across the ridge as we began to descend, swirling fires lit by the sinking sun. It was savagely beautiful, a sudden mix of terrifying weather and a sunset unlike those you will ever see in calmer skies.

It didn't take us long to realise the tent was much further away than we expected, so we opted for a long snow-slick bum slide to the valley floor. We rocketed down for maybe four hundred metres,

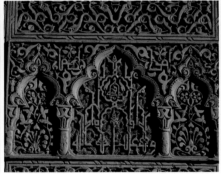

our ice axes serving as brakes and our whoops of joy echoing through the dusk. But by the time we reached the bottom, time, altitude and exertion had all taken their toll. We were utterly shattered. And the weather, having issued its warning, was no longer in the mood for play. We stumbled back towards the tent in darkness, and I felt an exhaustion I'd never known before. I collapsed several times into drifts of powder and lay there, feeling the snow blowing around my face and wanting nothing more than to close my eyes and fall asleep.

By the time we reached the tent it was black and our headlamps cast sad pools of light, just sufficient to see streaks of snow whistling past and a tent in danger of being blown away. With one of those desperate surges of energy you never know you have until you really need it, we spent a frantic hour tying extra guy lines and building a wall of rocks around the tent. Several times we were blown off our feet. Only when there were no more points to tie down and no more rocks to build the wall any higher with, did we collapse inside. It was a timely reminder of our altitude and the time of year. We had perhaps been a little naive.

Next morning we were up with the dawn and eager to escape the storm. Neither of us had slept well with the relentless banging of fabric and the deafening roar of wind, so packing was a bleary and uncoordinated stuffing of wet kit into rucksacks. We wrapped up well, and stepped out into the steely light of day. With backs to Mulhacén and the wind, we scuttled like guilty crabs, away from our mountain idyll turned hell-hole.

Back in Trevélez our elation was extreme. We celebrated with beers in a bar, our faces still raw from the wind, our minds alive with excitement. We re-lived the beauty and the moments of fear to make sure they were all real. We had done it. We had flown to an unknown part of Europe to climb an unfamiliar mountain with very little money and even less in the way of high-altitude experience. It had been a fantastic trip, accessible and adventurous, and just the right side of foolish.

But would you really want to do it? If you have never experienced profound solitude, the magic intensity of a winter Milky Way and a perfect frozen wilderness, then the answer should be yes. And if you want to know what it feels like to make fresh tracks through the snow to a country's highest peak, the entire range laid deserted beneath you, then again, the answer should be yes.

Mulhacén will not be the easiest challenge you'll ever set yourself but, as a perfect halfway-house between UK hills and the Alps, it's one you can do. Beg, borrow or even buy your kit for winter camping, get yourself the required winter skills and head for a challenge that'll leave you more satisfied than a fireside cat. At least until next time.

# LIGHT FANTASTIC

LIGHTWEIGHT TREKKING MEANS SAWN-OFF TOOTHBRUSHES, COLD NIGHTS AND FREEZE-DRIED FOOD, RIGHT? NOT IN SLOVENIA, ACCORDING TO BEN WINSTON.

Photography **Matthew Roberts**

**BIRTH OF A NATION**
November 1943 – Tito and Socialist Yugoslavia
April 1990 – Slovenia is first Yugoslav republic to hold free elections
December 1990 – 88 per cent of Slovenians vote for independence
June 1991 – Slovenia pulls out of Yugoslav Federation
June 1991 – Yugoslav army marches on Slovenia
July 1991 – Truce brokered by EU after 10 days of war and 66 deaths
Jan 1992 – Slovenia formally recognised
May 1992 – Slovenia admitted to the UN

Halfway along the three-day ridge.

# "LOSE WEIGHT NOW!
# Call 0800 672569."

It's the ultimate diet. Eat peas, blend nutrition drinks. Wrap your fat in cling film. Bounce, wobble and stretch into shape. Emulate the Lycra lady on the TV. Grunt, groan, suffer. Sit in a sauna. Try hypnosis. Fast. Strap on a muscle toner and jiggle till a six-pack emerges.

But I've got a better plan…

"LOSE WEIGHT NOW!" Unpack the tent, chuck out the sleeping bag, forget the stove and carry no food. Go walking. Go climb a mountain. Trek for weeks with just a day pack. Leave the crowds behind and stay in comfortable huts. Explore the mountains without the weight of camping. Come to Slovenia.

It's amazing what sunshine and traffic can do to your daydreams. We're stuck beneath a red light and I'm gazing unfocused at a faded orange sticker, lamp post shrapnel of guerrilla marketing. "LOSE WEIGHT NOW!" it implores, which, strangely, is why we're here in the first place, waiting, watching exhausts splutter and smog, browning up the air. It's hot and I'm restless, eager to get to Slovenia and start exploring one of Europe's finest ridge walks. There are some 165 mountain huts, refuges and bivouacs in the mountains of Slovenia, I'm told, so we've packed just a few bare essentials and some cash. We'll be living dawn and dusk at altitude; no plunging down at night and no struggling back up in the morning. It's going to be great, just as soon as – flash – we get our green light and go roaring off into Stansted airport.

"Just the one bag is it, sir?" Absolutely. One bag, one pair of boots, one waterproof jacket,

one toothbrush and a change of clothes. But she doesn't need to know all this, just that the 'sack weighs less than nine kilos and is too big (but only just) to be carried on as hand luggage. I'm proud of it – it took me 20 minutes to pack. Which is twice as long as it took to book the flight and half the time it took to get to the airport.

"Did you pack it yourself?" Yup. Small, isn't it? I've never travelled so light in my life. "Departure gate number 14, sir. Boarding time is 11am. Have a nice flight."

I do. I sit at the window and stare out at Europe, clear beneath. The Alps, mapped out in lines of sun and shadow, lead inexorably towards Slovenia. It's not somewhere I could have found on a map a couple of weeks ago, yet now I'm on my way there, flying east, following this great chain of peaks and the rumour that Slovenia is Europe's forgotten walking paradise.

Stamp, stamp, stamp, and – with walking companion Chris and photographer Matthew – I've arrived. It's eastern Europe, apparently, but all I can see is a border official who knows how to smile and a petrol station selling flowers. It's rather civilised. Not quite what I expected.

Lisa, the programme co-ordinator at Freedom of Slovenia (a tour operator, not a rebel faction), says surprise is a normal response. It's a common assumption that Slovenia is full of concrete apartment blocks and people saying 'Comrade', plus it's at war with Yugoslavia. It's none of these things, but a beautiful, peaceful country the size of Wales, covered in forest and mountains, and more influenced by western Europe than a bleak past of communism.

"It's a great country and the Slovenes are a fantastic people," Lisa assures us. "They love the outdoors and have superb facilities for everything – you can go climbing, caving, canoeing or horse riding. There's some serious mountaineering, and a whole selection of easy walks in the valleys. People

## CURRENCY

The Slovene currency is the tolar (SIT for short) and as we went to press there were 331 of them to the pound.

## USEFUL PHRASES

**Hello** – Zivio / Dober dan

**Goodbye** – Adios / Nasvidenje

**Cheers** – Na zdravje

**How far is it to the summit?** – Kako dalec je vrh?

**Please stop whipping my bottom with that birch stick** *(a traditional welcome to Triglav's summit)* – Prosim pocakajte, da vas bom krstil

Clockwise from top left: Andraz at home on a log; the dreaded garlic sausage; summit of Skrbina; turning for the hut; dorm; capital Ljubljana; Tolminski Kuk summit; head whole.

## WILDLIFE

Slovenia's huge forests are home to the European brown bear, deer, boar, chamois, wolf and lynx. The country also hosts 2,900 plant species, including a number not found anywhere else in the world.

call Slovenia 'the New Zealand of Europe', you know. You'll love it." I need to be careful. I have been known to fall heavily for countries like this.

The affair begins the following morning at the bottom of a very long, steep hill. A sadistic introduction, but with singing birds and scent of pine to help offset the pain of going uphill, it's not actually that bad. Andraz, our mountain guide, is taking us along the ridge south of Lake Bohinj for a couple of days to show us what's great about Slovenian walking. I discover the first bit as I pick up and sling on my 'sack.

I remove it immediately and put it back down. Then I pick it up and sling it back on. The lack of weight is such a novel feeling that I do it once more. With the boots now on my feet, the only kilos come from three litres of water and a few clothes. So within minutes I've buckled up and forgotten it's there. Which is just as well because the path is unashamed of gradients and goes straight up.

Pearls of sweat keep dribbling from eyebrows, falling through perspective from large to small and puffing into dusty ground. It's a hypnotic melody, this pace and perspiration – a view of shuffling feet, thighs tensing, undergrowth passing. I only realise a quarter day has passed when a new landscape materialises beneath me with a long drop to distant forests and a chocolate-box village in a clearing. We're at 1760m and, finally, on the ridge.

I stop, breathe deeply and register the view. It's expansive. But with a growl my stomach registers the unfilled space inside of me. We are carrying no lunch. Thankfully, Andraz is already leading us to salvation and a hut which must be close for there's a steady stream of people heading down, *Dober dan*-ing us 'good day'. They're a curious bunch, these Slovenian walkers: some wear boots and check shirts, some wear trainers. A couple of them are completely steaming: I can hear the beer fumes whistling from their pores. "It's a national holiday," Andraz says by way of explanation; then a concrete building looms over us. "People like to walk up here for lunch."

That's a liquid lunch, it seems, for the tables are covered in beer bottles and there's all manner of folk stood around having a good time. Grannies and young children, people dressed in sporty Lycra shorts and others in jeans; in Slovenia age, ability and lack of technical apparel are not impediments to reaching the 1800m

The sort of situation for which walking was invented...

contour. We choose a table and order four bowls of thick bean soup from world-renowned mountaineer Reinhold Messner, or at least someone who looks the part. Hot food for lunch, washed down with cups of tea while sat at a table and I'm beginning to see the civilised appeal of all this. Perhaps I could be converted.

After lunch the ridge runs away with itself over a range of mountains and we follow it loosely. At first I'm surprised we don't stick to the crest like glue, but then that's because doing so would commit us to well over a month of scrambling. Things are on a different scale out here. Instead we walk at an easy pace through a slowly changing landscape, the path supported by bits of wood and a cable where there's the slightest chance of getting a fear on, but mostly running fine and letting us stare at the view. Over to the north, away across Lake Bohinj, the Julian Alps draw clouds and shred them viciously over bare pinnacles. There are enormous faces of sheer or overhanging rock; saw-toothed ridges and inaccessible hanging valleys. Triglav, the country's highest summit, looks formidable.

All of which makes me glad to be where we are, following a ridge now rolling grassy green, now a broad but shattered spine of limestone; prehistory's bleached skeleton peeping through the earth. It's easy walking and yet the day is running long, so I'm also glad when we turn down a spur to another, this time wooden, mountain hut. Perched high above the lake, 10 hours and God knows how many miles from this morning, the day is drawing to a close. It's already dark in the valley and when the sun sets spectacularly, I realise smugly that this is a private viewing. Entry fee: 1500m of ascent. Red skies, night, and I'm utterly delighted. But I'm

### MOUNTAIN TEA
Every mountain hut serves mugs of their own tea, invariably containing lots of sugar. Hut guardians collect local flowers and herbs to flavour it, and you can be sure never to drink the same cup twice. Always delicious.

shattered too and so, after a fine meal and a long-awaited (and well-deserved) beer, I fall unconscious into bed.

Next morning we're beginning to slip into the natural rhythm of things and wake up at dawn. The birds are singing and there's a cloud inversion in the valley. As I stand watching the sun rise it strikes me that I've been living an industrial life for so long that I've forgotten what a beautiful time of day this is.

Late morning and the atmosphere is threatening. The clouds have rolled in and we're hidden in a world of fog, looming rock towers and wispy ghosts that play on the edge of my vision. I can sense steep drops all around and feel the exposure of a path I can no longer see.

When the clouds clear briefly we're revealed as insignificant figures in a vast corrie of scree and snow, huge cliffs above and steep, sweeping slopes beneath. We really are in a lonely spot. Strangely, I find myself missing the security of a tent on my back and the reassurance of self-sufficiency. But the pay-off is distance and speed, so before I've time to get truly scared in this remote corrie, we've reascended to the crest.

But this is not what I was expecting. The ridge has gone all narrow – too narrow – and the cloud clears on our right to leave the drop fully exposed. It's awesome. Awful, even. It's peering at me through my toes. Neck hairs prickle, adrenaline tingles in my blood.

Ba-dumph-ba-dumph-ba-dumph-ba-dumph. My heart seems to be threatening an exit via my ears.

Matthew and Chris are scared too. The three of us are moving like wooden puppets, putting so much effort into every move to make sure it's

Clockwise from left: high on the crest of the ridge; lush lower lands; adventure playground; Savica waterfall; simpleton gurn; caption not needed.

not our last. We pull and clamber, grasping at rocks. And then we come across a bottomless chute scattered with ball bearing pebbles. They clatter when disturbed: clatter and roll for perhaps a slow-motion millisecond or less before their metre-long chute runs out and…

Silence.

They disappear over the edge.

But Andraz is there – offering a hand and warm words of encouragement, telling us we can make it. He's right. It's not hard. It's just the drop. Which isn't really an issue unless we look at it too much or take a slip, but in doing neither we cross safely to a broad descent and a very few deep breaths. We're at a thank-you-I-believe-in-you-God wide col. It's all over.

The ridge loses its sting after that and I'm all elation and glee. Exhausted, maybe, but exhilarated too, yet even more pleased when we begin to descend and the clouds start to clear, exposing the true extent of the Julian Alps. This really is a magnificent place. But perhaps it has something to do with the way the sun keeps bursting through, exploding onto the scene with a fanfare of sunbeams, lighting this peak here, that orange limestone wall there, that great big multi-storey hut…

I do a double take. It's still there. Towering over the trees and visible for miles around, there's this stonking great building made entirely of wood. And it's where we're heading for the night, thankfully, for my feet are sore and my knees are threatening to seize up.

Click, the light goes out. Someone farts and we giggle. Puerile, I know, but then it's the end of a long day and we've put away a few beers. Besides, we are four men in a dorm.

It's not long before someone's snoring. I lie with my hands on my stomach, listening to the nasal orchestra and feeling the cool air breeze in through the window. It's the end of our walk. I'm shattered and a little melancholy, but can't get to sleep. Thoughts soon begin to swirl and memories run intertwined. There's that rucksack, incredibly small and still shrinking. Then there's the scramble and that awful drop. Things grow more fluid as I teeter on the edge of sleep, standing above that bottomless chute with all those rolling stones. I slip on a dream and tumble off down through the clouds, spinning, cruising in gently to land at the airport. Ha ha! The airport!

"Gate 14 sir. Have a nice flight…"

Parp.

# AMONG FRIENDS

A SIMPLE TWIST OF FATE TOOK THE WORK-WEARY
TOM HUTTON BACK TO THE PYRENEES, IN SEARCH
OF A LEGENDARY LOST MOUNTAIN.

Pictures **Tom Hutton**

I drank in the scenery and knew I'd been away too long – far too long. In whichever direction I gazed, my eyes came to rest upon familiar old friends: rugged limestone cliffs, razor-sharp arêtes, thrusting pinnacles that jutted abruptly into a deep blue sky. In the distance, the high peaks of the Pyrenees raised their snow-capped heads boldly above the immediate landscape and, in the valley far below, the rusty colours of autumn trees closeted the frantic gushing of a raging mountain stream. It was good to be back.

The lost mountain, found.
On the summit of Mont Perdu.

The long haul up from the Pineta Valley.

The Anisclo Canyon swallows the sunshine.

It happens to us all. Somehow, immersed in the hustle and bustle of everyday life, we lose touch with the things we love. The lifestyle that we protect so fiercely keeps us from doing the very things we created that lifestyle for. It happened to me last year and, if it hadn't been for a chance meeting in a local pub with an old friend of the human variety, I would probably still be up to my neck in normality. "I really fancy a week in the Pyrenees," John suddenly announced as we sat lamenting the things we should have done that summer. "Really?" I replied, almost shocked by fact that such an exciting yet serious proposition could actually be made so lightly. I gave no more than a few seconds' thought to the practicalities of this unexpected opportunity and replied, without daring to consider any potential obstacles, "When shall we go?"

The rest, as they say, is history. From my perch high above the Ordesa Canyon – a world heritage site and, to my mind, one of the true natural wonders of the world – it would have been difficult to imagine a more fortuitous twist of fate. Piles of professional junk that had been thrown carelessly down on the floor of my overworked mind were now effortlessly tidied away. I was finally back in the mountains and, boy, it felt good!

If it's walking rather than mountaineering that you're after, summer in the Pyrenees is about as good as it gets. Imagine the Scottish Highlands with reasonably predictable weather, well-marked trails and peaks that measure in metres as much as most Munros do in feet. Add to that an excellent network of refuges which will happily provide all your dietary requirements and a five- or six-day trek becomes a comfortable reality with little more than a day pack to weigh you down.

At our next and final planning meeting, it became obvious that John had really done his homework and he was quick to volunteer a list of the places that he wanted to see. It read like an honours list of the area: the breathtaking Ordesa Canyon, the instantly recognisable Breche de Rolande and, of course, Mont Perdu, the infamous lost mountain of the Pyrenees and, at 3355m, the highest limestone summit in Europe. An e-mail to Pyrenean Mountain Tours, specialists in all types of Pyrenean capers, revealed that they could not only advise us on routes and so on, but also book the refuges for us, drop us at a convenient start point and collect us once we'd finished. They've been providing this kind of support for self-guided trips for some time and, as the Pyrenees are generally a little more user-friendly than the Alps, they've become incredibly popular. With the planning taken care of, we had little more to do than to sit back and count down the days until we left.

Fortunately, time flies when you're busy and, in

Near the Col des Tentes.

what seemed like no time at all, we were sat in the bar of the Hotel Cimes, in the centre of the beautiful village of Luz-St-Saveur, poring over maps and talking through the route. The planning had been meticulous and we retired happy; tomorrow we would be back in the mountains, among friends.

If there was one highlight of the first day, it was the silence, the deafening silence. It seemed to close in on us from all sides and we somehow managed to walk in time with it. We viewed the Cirque de Gavarnie, an impenetrable bastion of broken rock, from an airy viewpoint, walked to its base to study Europe's highest waterfall and then wound our way up the hillside on a narrow twisting path that seemed to carve an impossible pass through a sheer wall of rock. The whole day was indeed spectacular but the silence made the deepest impression.

From Espugettes, we started climbing before dawn and, after a tough but thankfully cool pull over the Horquette d'Allans, we took a long break in the first rays of morning sunshine. Izards, the Pyrenean version of chamois, darted about in the valley below and countless marmots, comical creatures that resemble a rotund and cuddly cross between a teddy bear and a badger, sunbathed on rocks. Griffon vultures circled overhead and wisps of misty cloud danced nimbly among the surrounding peaks. The scenery, it seemed, just kept getting better; but the best was still to come.

Nicknamed the lost mountain, Mont Perdu (or Monte Perdido from the Spanish side) is hidden on both sides of the French/Spanish border by a plethora of surrounding peaks. It takes considerable effort to just view her snow-covered slopes, let alone climb them; yet many still make the pilgrimage. From the Col du Tuqueroye we saw why. Cresting a narrow couloir full of jumbled boulders and treacherous scree, we gazed upon her for the first time. Her daunting northern flanks towered majestically above the valley; at her feet a small mountain lake glowed a shade of blue that was almost alive. We ate lunch in her presence before continuing. We were to become better acquainted in a few days' time.

Day three went horribly wrong. We knew we had a big climb – 1300m to be precise – and we knew the sun was going to be on our backs for most of it, so we planned an early start. Annoyingly, we overslept! It was an expensive mistake and we were forced to toil, painfully slowly, up the steep hillside in the full strength of the morning sun. Brief respite came in the form of a small waterfall but it was scant consolation for four hours of intense labour; and by the time we hit the top, we knew we had little left to give that day. Fortunately the going eased and we enjoyed some relatively gentle walking for the remainder

Making steady progress in the Ordesa Canyon.

# I DREAM OF MOUNTAINS AND VALLEYS, OF CANYONS AND STREAMS, OF SUNRISE AND SUNSET AND OF THE MILES IN BETWEEN

The author's mountain motivation

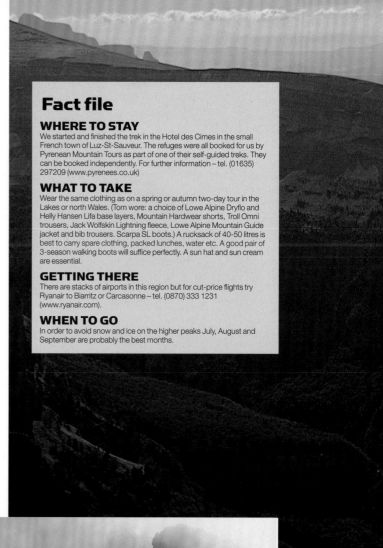

of the journey to the Goriz Hut. Goriz was to be our home for the next two nights and the base camp for our summit attempt in the morning. Dehydrated, tired and slightly apprehensive, we drank copious amounts of water, packed our bags, ate a pretty hearty meal and then retired early – we were unlikely to make the same mistake twice!

It was still dark as we prised ourselves out of the refuge. We followed the narrow beams of our trusty Petzls over the lower slopes with our eyes peeled for a narrow gully on the right. We found it, scrambled to its top and put our trekking poles on our bags. We had decided upon a bolder, scrambling route to the summit and it started here. We cleared the first of many steep but juggy rock bands and then stopped at the top to put away a few bars of chocolate and watch the sun as it peeked over the eastern horizon.

The route was a definite winner. The scrambling was reasonably easy – no worse than British Grade 1 – although in places it was fairly exposed. A rocky ridgeline gave us our first sight of the summit and we committed to memory the topography of the mountain, taking note of the number of remaining rock bands and the cleanest lines between them. It was to prove a worthwhile measure; the final move on the final scramble turned out to be the crux of the whole route – a difficult mantle that would be almost impossible to reverse. I have a rule when scrambling in unfamiliar territory: I never climb up what I can't climb down. We needed to be sure that, whatever happened, once we were over this section we would meet no further obstacles. Armed with some degree of foresight (and a lot of luck) we pressed on; our calculations were correct and 15 minutes later we sat on the summit with grins from ear to ear. We shook hands, took the obligatory photos and then set off down the main path – there was no way we were going to descend via the approach route. Three hours later we were back at the refuge. With the climb under our belts, the main objective of the trip had been achieved and it wasn't even lunchtime!

## Fact file

### WHERE TO STAY
We started and finished the trek in the Hotel des Cimes in the small French town of Luz-St-Sauveur. The refuges were all booked for us by Pyrenean Mountain Tours as part of one of their self-guided treks. They can be booked independently. For further information – tel. (01635) 297209 (www.pyrenees.co.uk)

### WHAT TO TAKE
Wear the same clothing as on a spring or autumn two-day tour in the Lakes or north Wales. (Tom wore: a choice of Lowe Alpine Dryflo and Helly Hansen Lifa base layers, Mountain Hardwear shorts, Troll Omni trousers, Jack Wolfskin Lightning fleece, Lowe Alpine Mountain Guide jacket and bib trousers. Scarpa SL boots.) A rucksack of 40-50 litres is best to carry spare clothing, packed lunches, water etc. A good pair of 3-season walking boots will suffice perfectly. A sun hat and sun cream are essential.

### GETTING THERE
There are stacks of airports in this region but for cut-price flights try Ryanair to Biarritz or Carcasonne – tel. (0870) 333 1231 (www.ryanair.com).

### WHEN TO GO
In order to avoid snow and ice on the higher peaks July, August and September are probably the best months.

The Horquettes d'Allans: here be marmots!

In the Ordesa Canyon, far from the nearest photocopier.

After a celebratory beer we decided it was pointless staying another night at Goriz. There was a refuge in the tiny town of Torla at the bottom of the valley. If we walked out that afternoon we'd be able to enjoy a comfortable night in civilisation before tackling the Breche de Rolande the next day. If all went according to plan, we'd finish a day early; if it didn't, we had a contingency day and that might prove useful if the weather broke.

Our new schedule left us with two days' walking in one day and we certainly knew about it by the time we made the bottom. It was worth it, though; Torla was delightful, the refuge comfortable and a few glasses of San Miguel never hurt anybody. We had another big day ahead though, and this meant another early night.

Again, we set off in darkness but the huge climb up from the Ordesa Canyon proved a lot easier than we were expecting. If Mont Perdu was the main course, then the next section was, without a doubt, the sweetest dessert we could have ever asked for. A narrow path ran along a precarious terrace a few metres beneath the clifftops. Sculpted overhangs, brightly coloured by natural minerals, offered shade from the relentless Spanish sun and, to our right, the ground dropped away, an almost sheer 1000m to the valley floor.

Mile after mile, the narrow walkway traversed the wall of rock. The drop to the right seemed to steepen with almost every step and the foreground changed repeatedly as pinnacle after broken pinnacle made a defiant stand against the ceaseless erosion of time. Sadly it came to an end and, after a tough scramble over a huge plateau of limestone pavement, we started climbing again. This foray took us to the Breche de Rolande – a deeply cloven pass in a formidable wall of rock. We could see it for some time but, as with many landmarks in the hills, it never seemed to get any closer. Eventually, after another fight with gravity and scree, working together in perfect harmony, we made the Breche. We ate lunch, then said our goodbyes to the impressive range of Spanish peaks that had been our home for the last few days. We reminded ourselves to greet our fellow walkers in French instead of Spanish, then reluctantly began the final descent.

Two hours later, sheltered from an ever-increasing wind in the Col du Tentes, we ate the last of our food and, with rapidly numbing fingers, I attempted to pen a final tribute to the mountains. Looking around, I realised what a thankless task it was; the pen may well be mightier than the sword, but some things in life simply defy description. Eleanor Roosevelt came closer than most when she said "only true friends leave a footprint on your heart." Somehow, to me, that seemed appropriate!

# WOT? NO FLAMENCO?

MAYBE THE BEARS ATE THE DANCERS. THIS IS SOMIEDO NATURAL PARK, WHERE THE LOCALS CARE AS MUCH ABOUT BULLFIGHTING AND FEISTILY-STRUMMED GUITARS AS A SCOTTISH HILL FARMER DOES CROQUET AND CREAM TEAS…

Words **Chritian Walsh**
Pictures **Josép Perez Gonzalez & Christian Walsh**

S deep within the Cordillera Cantabrica mountain range in north-west Spain is the last of western Europe's truly wild landscapes, the Somiedo Natural Park. Long overlooked by walkers, and far too remote for casual tourists, conservationists are understandably protective of this 30,000 hectares of jagged peaks and forested valleys. A mythical landscape that has changed little since Palaeolithic times, the misty lakes of Saliencia and the Valle de Lago are encircled by 2000m rock faces. With few roads and even fewer inhabitants – save shrinking mining and herding communities – the forests are alive with plants and wildlife unique to this region. But the grey wolf and mountain pansy are not the only inhabitants of the Somiedo wilderness. 'Take care,' warned my Spanish guidebook, 'this land is bear country.'

Somiedo is a haven for around 100 Iberian brown bears. Once plentiful in Europe, the bears have almost been hunted out of western Europe altogether (it is estimated that around 10 still live in the Pyrenees, while the rest can be found in Central Europe, Russia and Central Asia). With only 80 people living in Pola de Somiedo, the largest human settlement in the area, odds were in favour of us encountering a bear before we met the locals.

Poring over our maps in a cosy London flat, Josép and I reminded ourselves that many epic journeys are launched in search of some beast or other. There was Jason and the Golden Fleece, Captain Ahab and Moby Dick, Bruce Chatwin and the Patagonian sloth. Now the eyes of history were upon us and our search for the elusive (and extremely aggressive) Iberian brown bear. And if we didn't find it, at least we would have had a jolly good walk.

Below: Splendid isolation – the Lago del Valle.

Above: Shepherds delight in a braña with a view

Below: a hard day's nap on the route to La Pornacal.

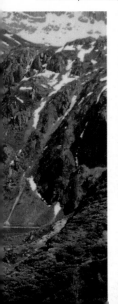

They look Nepalese, but these houses are typically Asturian.

The soul of Somiedo is in the high valleys around Lago Calabazosa.

We chose Somiedo because we were looking for somewhere remote to walk. With two of Spain's hiking autobahns – the immensely popular Picos de Europa and the Santiago Way – just down the road, Somiedo is like one of those magical corners of wasteland that thrive in the heart of a 'spaghetti junction', unspoilt and wild.

With stormy weather regularly coming off the Atlantic, the outlook for the week was wet with cold winds and the possibility of snow higher up. While thick snow is common until the end of April, the area is equally notorious for its humidity. It was destined to be one of those stop-start hikes: stripping down to a T-shirt one minute then hurriedly throwing on waterproofs the next. In a word, sweaty.

Arriving in Oviedo, 200km from the park, we had entered what was once the capital of the Asturian kingdom. In the 10th century, Asturias was the only Christian kingdom in Spain to drive back the Moorish invaders. Even the influence of Franco and the civil war were hardly felt in these snowbound valleys. A proud people who like the saying: 'To be Spanish is an honour, to be Asturian is a title.'

Almost as soon as the bus left the suburbs of Oviedo we entered a series of deep lush valleys. The road followed a river then ascended, zigzagging through open grasslands until we reached a plateau. On either side were narrow jagged ridges, whittled down by strong winds and rain. The road descended through miniature woods that huddled against the rock. We passed clusters of cottages and strange wooden huts on stilts called horreas inside which corn is laid to dry well away from the humid earth. Raised off the ground by four megalithic stone plinths, with a narrow balcony running around the outside, horreas look strangely eastern, a cross between a jungle hut and a pagoda.

On first appearances, Pola de Somiedo is a surprisingly featureless village where locals from around the valley congregate to drink red wine and catch up on gossip. A photocopy pinned to the bar door notified the community that last night Señor So-and-so joined the Lord in his 93rd year. I mentally adjusted the bears versus humans score. They would soon outnumber the population 2:1.

We lunched on an explosive mixture of local cider and Asturian favana – pieces of pig in a delicious flageolet bean stew. Outside, the bursts of sunshine grew more infrequent as rain clouds built up behind the mountains like a dark army. A mountain of a man came teetering down the road, balanced incongruously on a pair of uncomfortable-looking clogs. On the soles of this unlikely footwear are three-inch-long wooden prongs which force anyone wearing them to shuffle effeminately. Looking around the bar I

# A MOUNTAIN OF A MAN CAME TEETERING DOWN THE ROAD, BALANCED INCONGRUOUSLY ON A PAIR OF UNCOMFORTABLE-LOOKING CLOGS

We recommend you purchase your footwear outside the park!

The village of Valle del Lago makes an idyllic base for day treks.

Sudden mists engulf the luxuriant valleys.

Brañas offer shelter and a few bones to chew on if supplies are low.

realised everyone – men, women and children – was wearing them. That night we realised their value as we skidded through the cow muck on the way back to the guest house.

The next day we set off from La Peral, a little way south along the main road from Pola de Somiedo. The route is easy, climbing from 1300 to 1800 metres where there is a sensational 360° panorama of snow-capped mountains. The bristling peaks of the Picos de Europa were clearly visible to the west. The valley here is largely heath with a smattering of twisted woods. The path leads clearly down the opposite valley until you reach a huddle of primitive-looking thatched cottages. This is La Pornacal, and the deserted cottages are another part of the fascinating cultural puzzle of Somiedo. There are about 30 stonewalled houses in this isolated valley, each one with a five foot wooden door which is secured with a hefty padlock. There are no windows, and a thatched roof overhangs the cottage walls like a great mop of hair. The overall image is idyllic: grassy paths, little paddocks and a stream gurgling beneath miniature stone bridges – this is Asterixville.

But it is not really a village. There are no communal buildings – no church or town hall or village store. This is the largest of many brañas that can be found in the high pastures around Somiedo. They were originally built for shepherds who led their flocks hundreds of miles from the dry regions of Extramadura, bordering Portugal, to graze in these mountains during the summer. This practice of transhumance continued for hundreds of years and some farmers we met still remembered the arrival of these semi-nomads each year. The trip from central Spain was hard on the animals, and the trains of sheep were accompanied by hovering vultures ready to pick up scraps. A few farmers from Extramadura

still make the trip, in trucks these days. Some locals use the brañas to stay overnight when their herds of vaca roxa, or Asturian red cow, need a good feed.

Having passed through La Pornacal, the path descended gradually and the heath turned into luxuriant pasture hemmed in by disorderly hedgerows. Almost tropical in appearance, this narrow, humid valley exploded with new growth. The valley opened up and so did the clouds. Our first experience of the changeability of Asturian weather was borne heroically (cheered by the knowledge that we only had an hour left before we reached the end of the trail at Villar de Vildas). Walking into the village, we instantly wished we were staying here instead of the crossroads town of Pola de Somiedo. Donkeys brayed from underneath wooden balconies. Whole corn hung in bunches from ornate horreas, and red cows were hustled into ancient barns by old men clip-clopping in their wooden stilettos.

Taking shelter in the village bar, I asked the proprietor if he had seen any bears recently. He threw up his hands in excitement and asked me if I wanted to see his prints. ("Prints!" I thought. "Could it be? A dusty box of brittle photographs; men holding macabre hunt-trophies, mothers and cubs rolling in the snow at the mouth of their lair, a severed human forearm found in a bear's stomach. Yes! Lead me to them!"). Into the dining room we hurried and there it was, on the wall. The proprietor beamed proudly as he pointed to a depressingly familiar poster. The same tourist board poster of a suspiciously rigid bear that we had seen in every restaurant, shop and lodge since arriving 48 hours ago.

After Pola de Somiedo our next base was the more isolated and altogether more pleasing village, Valle de Lago. We chose the Auterio guest house, a converted stable on the far side of the village run by an elderly farmer and his wife. It seemed we had found our ideal setting; a fire-lit mountain dwelling in which walnut-faced shepherds would entertain us with stories of Asturian legend.

The next day we headed down the Valle de Lago towards the Lago del Valle (logical, if unimaginative). To either side of the path flat pastures fed from a river that flowed the length of the valley. The springy meadow grass was flecked with bright yellow centaury. High paths led to hidden plateaux, barren, mystical and deserted. We saw several herds of wild chamois perched on the abrupt ridges hundreds of feet above our trail.

The glacial lakes of Saliencia form a vast arena whose sheer sides are streaked with snow and fallen rock. Sudden mists would descend over the higher lakes of Cueva and Calabazosa (1500m) and then disappear just as quickly. Standing alone in this massive crater, I felt as if I was in place where things still happen that modern people have forgotten long ago. If I could pinpoint the soul of Somiedo, it would be here.

An unplanned detour led us into a beech wood. Overhead, grey-green lichen hung in swathes from grotesquely gnarled branches. The path was thrown into deeper shadow as the trees on either side of us embraced and formed a tunnel. Little sun could get through the tangle and the air became thicker and more humid as we progressed. Although it was May there were piles of last year's leaves on the ground and at times the path was hard to see.

We walked as stealthily as possible, binoculars and cameras at the ready, determined to see the wildlife before we scared it away. That morning Señor Auterio told us that at this time of the year all the animals would be in the wood. All? If there ever were a place to catch a bear unawares, it was here. I wished that Josép was carrying Señora Auterio's homemade chorizo sausage, not me.

Bears are only aggressive if they feel threatened. Unfortunately they have terrible eyesight so they always feel threatened. If you see one across the plain, no problem. If you stumble across one at close range, say in a wood… problem. We decided to skip our usual postprandial snooze when we discovered a set of massive paw prints. The wood was getting darker and the path was getting fainter. Soon we were lost.

For just over an hour we stumbled through the dense trees. The binoculars had been packed away, and for the first time in a week our witty banter had dried up. After four hours we came out the other side, relieved and exhausted. We were so busy congratulating each other, we didn't see the park guard. He had a vicious-looking rifle slung over his shoulder.

"Where have you just come from?" he quizzed us sharply. "Have you been through the forest?" It turned out we had walked through a protected area. Fortunately he could see we were hopeless specimens and gently lectured us on the principles of conservation. Besides, he added, walking in the woods could be dangerous.

As he turned to leave I saw several rounds of ammunition belted around his waist. "Señor," I asked in bad Spanish, "what's the gun for?"

"Protection," he said, and disappeared into the wood.

We never saw any bears in Somiedo. What we did see was a place that is quintessentially Spanish, and yet somewhere that tourists probably wouldn't recognise as being Spanish. Locked within an ancient, timeless landscape is a population that feels as alien to paella, bullfights and flamenco as a Hebridean does to Cornish cream teas, croquet and the Changing of the Guard. My companion, a native Catalan, was as excited as I was to find a cider-brewing, clog-wearing community who spoke a mixture of Spanish and Gaelic, and that found the two of us as odd and funny as we found them.

# Fact file

## WHEN TO GO
Higher altitudes are snowbound from November until late April. Some of the roads might also be impassable during winter. June to September is the best time for reliable weather – little rain and plenty of sun.

## GETTING THERE
Iberia flies direct to Oviedo – tel. (0845) 601 2854 (but this can be pricy). Cheaper to fly to Madrid and take the train. From Barcelona the overnight train only costs around £30 return. From Oviedo a bus leaves for Pola de Somiedo at 10am every day of the week. If you decide to follow our recommended route, then you can catch a taxi from Pola to the start of the trek at Saliencia for around £10. If you don't fancy working that hard, Discovery Travel do guided and self-guided hols in the area –  tel. (01904) 766564 or email info@discoverytravel.co.uk

## GETTING AROUND
A car is very useful for exploring this region thoroughly. You can hire a car in Oviedo with a valid driving licence. If you don't mind hanging around on street corners, there are plenty of locals happy to give you a lift from one village to the next. We made do without a car, combining hitching with fairly inconsistent public transport.

## WHERE TO STAY
There are several guest houses in each of the villages. They are listed in a brochure provided by the excellent tourist office in Pola de Somiedo. A double room with bathroom cost a meagre £7-8 a night. You can buy provisions in Pola although it would be marginally more economical to stock up in Oviedo beforehand. We highly recommend Auteirio guest house for its charming location and owners.

## VISAS, MONEY & INSURANCE
You don't need a visa to enter Spain if you are coming from the UK. There is a bank in Pola that accepts Visa transactions and changes traveller's cheques. Insurance for all occurrences should be arranged prior to leaving, including rescue and medical insurance.

## GEAR, GUIDES & GUIDEBOOKS
No climbing gear is needed unless you plan to walk in Somiedo during winter when there is much snow and ice. Otherwise take water- and windproofs. It can suddenly turn chilly, even on a sunny day, so bring a fleece; and remember some head protection.

Hiring a guide is unnecessary, and maps can be bought in Pola. All trails are well marked, and a Spanish topographical map of the area can be bought in major travel shops in the UK. If you speak Spanish and can't get hold of the excellent Parque Natural de Somiedo (Green Guides collection, written by Enric Balasch Blanch) it too is sold in guest houses and shops in and around Pola de Somiedo. Otherwise Lonely Planet's Walking in Spain gives a good overview of the main walks.

## The route
Most guidebooks feature day walks using a fixed base. Here is a four-day continuous trek that we tried and tested to save you backtracking.

**Day 1:** Start your trek in Saliencia where you can spend the night. From here walk via the lakes of La Cueva and Calabazosa to Valle de Lago – a good day's walk.

**Day 2:** Take the track up to the Brañas de Sousas, and continue south along a series of peaks of around 2000m until you descend into the town of Puerto de Somiedo.

**Day 3:** Take the road for just over a mile till you arrive at La Peral. From here follow the trail towards the Brañas La Pornacal and continue until you enter the village of Villar de Vildas.

**Day 4:** A bus leaves for Oviedo every morning.

# WISH IT WAS STILL WINTER?

Snow. Mountains. And here, at 1600m, we were actually allowed to play on them...

SICK OF THE SUCKING BOGS OF BRITISH SPRING?

PHOTOGRAPHY **ITALY** TOM BAILEY **MALLORCA** MATTHEW ROBERTS

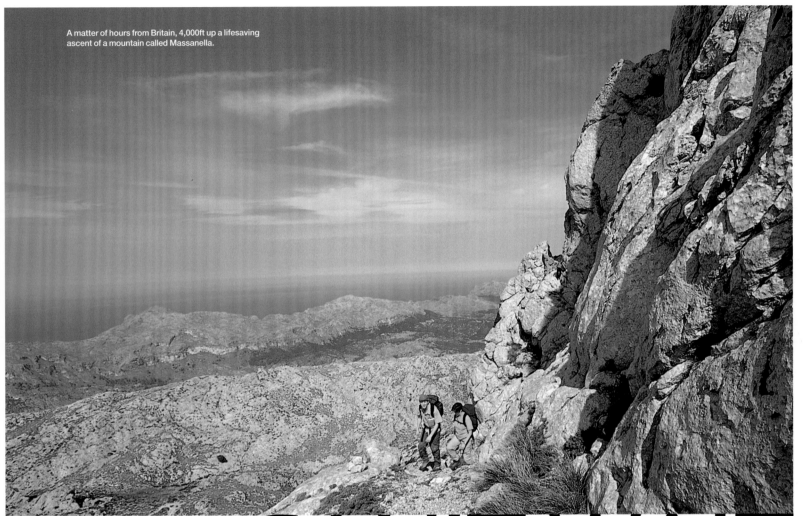

A matter of hours from Britain, 4,000ft up a lifesaving ascent of a mountain called Massanella.

# CAN'T WAIT FOR SUMMER?

**BEN WINSTON** AND **GUY PROCTER** FIND EUROPE OFFERS AFFORDABLE ESCAPE ROUTES FOR ANY OCCASION. YOU EVEN GET TO PICK YOUR FAVOURITE SEASON.

A moment of almost British clarity on top of Monte Corchia.

## ITALY

Winter; it's the season of discontent. Snow, rain, high winds and short days – everything about it says run away. Yet I love it; always have. I could never give up such classic moments as the 'well-earned pint'; wet, knackered and steaming slowly dry in the corner of a cosy pub. Or even the 'Ohmygodwillyoulookatthat!' sensation you get when the clouds clear on the top of a snowy Munro. So you can imagine how I felt when, part way through this season of axes and crampons, someone told me that, er… sorry, but there's a problem with the countryside – you can't go and play any more.

That first weekend was bad but bearable: I waxed my boots with such sad longing that they went uselessly soft. The weekend after was harder: I began a search for local tower blocks and flights of stairs to restlessly climb and descend. By the third weekend, with snows flurrying and Britain having some of its best winter weather for centuries, I was apoplectic with frustration. It was time for action.

Out came the guidebooks, on went the computer and by the end of the day I was set to be a mountain man again – one half of the Trail office was booked on a cheap flight for Italy's Apuan Alps. We'd not heard of them either but, just a short stretch north of Pisa, within sight of the Med and rising to almost 2000m, they looked like they might exactly be what we were looking for. Dramatically peaked, cleft by deep valleys, centred around a 30km ridge and popularly described as 'dolomitic', they once gave Michelangelo the marble for his most famous works. But we were going for neither art nor history – we going to play in the snow.

## MALLORCA

This should have been Scafell Pike. Over there by Sprinkling Tarn should have been our base camp – the launch pad for a long weekend unlocking the secrets of the massif around England's highest peak.

It was meant to be a big hello to spring – glorious spring; the thin end of summer's wedge and the official start of wild camping.

Ah, the optimism of the summer-lover. Blame it on the sunshine. Blame it on the moonlight. Blame it on the boogie – it wouldn't have been like that at all. Even if the fells hadn't been debarred by foot-and-mouth, the snow that lay thick on the peg-bendingly frozen ground would have made any camping trip a feat of endurance.

Thus a happy accident amid national heartache saw me

Mallorca-bound. Mallorca, where even in March the first breath of summer was causing mass narcolepsy among cats and honey-coloured Mediterranean girls to go down another blouse button.

I'm no travel expert, and so it was with constant amazement that I found how cheap and genuinely easy it is to steer oneself plum into the middle of an English summer, adrift off the west coast of Spain. Let's go…

# The first 24 hours… (ITALY)

She must be over 80 and she's knocking back stiff black espressos like there's no tomorrow, which there won't be, if she's not careful. I consider warning her about caffeine-induced heart attacks but then realise she's Italian, was probably breast-fed the stuff and could no doubt bolt up the hill we are due to climb in the time it takes to tie my laces.

We never get to find out, though – she's off out the door before we reach the bottom of our short, sharp shots, although I reckon it would be a close race because by then we're buzzing too. So much so that the first hill, although only slightly off-vertical, is dispatched with such speed that we find ourselves way up and teetering on a ridge before we even know what's happening.

Before us is a scene straight out of an improbable Bavarian kid's book: fairytale towers asserting stubborn independence; enormous (and I mean *enormous*) limestone faces standing solemn, parentlike; and gravity, that irresistible old piper, asserting its scree slope authority. It's a dramatic change from the marble landscape of Levigliani where the cliffs are now all quarries, but we hardly notice, such is the distorting effect of the caffeine.

The *rifugio*, in this strange world of zip and haste, is but a nanosecond further on, although it's a beautiful nanosecond filled with pine woods and a lone hunting goshawk. We belt on, wave a hasty hellogoodbye to the stout Italian guardian as we pass – a man who, we can see from the expression on his face, needs only a mountain hut, a dog and an axe to attain enlightenment – and roar on up Monte Corchia.

We're just full of energy and scratch speedily along a ridge with a leftward drop that would take us back to the wired granny's garden in Levigliani. On the right the cloud keeps clearing to slap us with a staggering view of tomorrow's awesome target – the huge bulk of Pania della Croce (1858m).

As the 1676m summit approaches time begins to slow, the coffee rush comes to an end and I judder back down into the real world, largely intact although noticeably more nervous than when I was last here, at breakfast. Corchia, however, is too broad a peak to give you the willies and its beauty leaves little space for anything but endless repetitions of the word "Wow!", even if my companions seem not quite so verbally crippled and protest at what is becoming a rather tedious monologue.

Back at base the serene Italian cooks up a dinner scene leading to a *waffer theen mint* moment. It's followed by a solid night of *rifugio* comfort (complete with a pint – well, 500cl – and a roaring wood, er… burner), that sets us up perfectly for when we plod out in the rain for the summit of the Pania – the most famous mountain in the Alpi Apuani.

## POSTCARD

Guy,

We're standing at 1676m, the clouds have broken up and taken to billowing spectacularly off the peaks. The sun is backlighting everything, the distant Med is sparkling and Tom is gibbering because I've had to hide his film (so there's some left for tomorrow). Have you found a deckchair hire yet?

Ben

# The first 24 hours... (MALLORCA)

By Mallorca I mean of course that Mallorca – better known as Majorca, the second home of chip-fed British families in search of beaches and the holy mysteries of the lager coma.

A hundred kilometres wide and 75 north to south, this roughly diamond-shaped island is the largest of the Balearics. Luckily, the island splits nicely in two: the plains and beaches of the south for the package crowd, and the genuinely lovely, mountainous north for walkers. Just over two hours' plane journey away, Mallorca's mountains are best in April, when the vegetation is still green and the temperatures perfect for summer-style walking. All the best routes are in the mountain range called the Serra Tramuntana, which runs across the north edge of the island, reaching a high point for walkers in Massanella, 1367m (4,484ft) – 80ft higher than Ben Nevis. (Puig Major is the island's highest point at 1,447m but it's been closed for military use.)

But how good is Mallorca's best? We headed for Valldemossa after scouring the small ads for accommodation in Trail and Country Walking magazines. Again, this was a lucky accident – Valldemossa is actually in the Tramuntana, so the walking's right there, and the small town itself is utterly Mediterranean and unspoilt.

So picture the scene: after an evening flight from cold, plague-ridden Britain, we've been disinfected, picked up a car with a daily hire cost about the same as a mountain bike in the Lake District, and driven the half hour from twinkling Palma to the dark quiet of Valldemossa. Tomorrow, we walk!

Our first day is spent walking on our landlady's recommendation (always a good idea in a strange country). It's called the Archduke's Path, and rises from a back street into the low woods that cover the lower slopes. It's our first sight, smell and sound of the place and it's beguiling.

Our summery clothes no longer feel like costumes as we climb the loose, rubbly path. The higher we go, the more boulders lie around – bone dry limestone the texture of cellulite which is perfect for smeary, finger-parching scrambles.

The forest climb lasts an hour, then it's out onto an airy ledge giving our first real view. Expecting desert, my eyes swim with the dark blue of the sea (visible at an angle of about 45° below), the vivid green of the plains and the wispy white outcrops of limestone. A few swimming pools gleam. It's a bit like the view of earth from space.

The Archduke's path is like a mini Hadrian's Wall – a track the eponymous nobleman would ride for the simple pleasure of the views. As the track veers right to return to Valldemossa, we leave it for a there-and-back to our first summit – a pleasure denied for weeks in Britain. It's called Teix (1062m/3,483ft) and the alternately rocky and heathy path soon becomes a solid rock clamber to the top. A few chalky layers of haze, some blond cliffs rising from forest like giant Stanage Edges, sea in three directions and mountains trailing off in the direction of tomorrow... That's *better*.

On the way to our first summit in weeks – Teix (1062m/3,483ft).

## POSTCARD

Ben,

It's like a giant limestone Dales round here – the weather's perfect for walking and we've had a foretaste of a great summer's walking. Plus the locals are charitable. This is us in the restaurant:

"[confidently] Dos cerveza por favor"

"But there are three of you?"

"Er, yeah, three please. Gracias."

"You're welcome"

We're so winning.

Guy

# The second 24 hours… (ITALY)

For reasons alien to rivers and those who seek the line of least resistance, we've chosen route 125 to take us around the flank of the Pania before we make our summit attempt.

You see, the red dotted lines denote 'Sentiero Difficile'. Translation: 'fun footpath'. There are snow slicks and scrambling as we clamber around the base of enormous crags, running over the bits where stone chutes empty their lethal cargo into the abyss below. To complete the scene we get some of those great British 'clearing in the cloud' moments when a landscape momentarily materialises way beneath our feet.

In our eagerness we try to hurry the summit by leaving the footpath, which has turned into a regal series of pure marble steps, and scoot off along an obvious ridge. On the map it's marked as broad, with cliffs on one side, but in reality it grows far too airy too quickly, and we're turned back by a series of rock centurions rising decisively from mist.

Instead, in the snow bowl of the mountain's north face, we strap on crampons and whip axes from our 'sacks. The feeling is one of great adventure, the sensation of being a long way from anywhere on the side of a mighty and crag-strewn mountain. But then disaster strikes. Maria is struck by an excruciating pain in the lower back, doubles over and dies. Or she would have, had her condition been as serious as Pania's north face feels, which thankfully it wasn't.

Still, as she crumples into a heap we realise quite how far from help we are. It also strikes me that we cannot summon a helicopter with a vocabulary consisting largely of 'ravioli', 'tiramisu' or 'proscuttio', no matter how emphatic the pronunciation, and we are now in trouble. Doggedly we manage to hobble to the nearest rifugio where, after a rest and copious cups of instant cappuccino, Maria mercifully recovers. But our second assault on Pania has been thwarted…

In spite of a tantalising evening where the clouds clear to show us what we've been missing, plus the true scale of Pania's north face and a small avalanche, by the time morning comes it's all fugged up again. The snow is the consistency of Slush Puppie and the conditions a true whiteout, but a line of footprints leads us safely to the summit ridge. I pray for clarity and thereby prove the irrefutable fact that: a) there is no God, or b) if there is a God then He doesn't like me.

Whichever, by the time we reach the large metal cross whistling on the top we know we are in for that quintessentially British summit experience – the viewless lunch. But it doesn't matter because all the hard work and adventure that's brought us to this point, plus the ache in our legs and our sore shoulders, makes this moment infinitely worthwhile. We're well wrapped up against disappointment in the electric air of summit elation.

Snow fun in the fog.

The spectacular rifugio Rossi.

It's rustic, but comfort indeed.

### POSTCARD

Guy!
We've found winter! We're playing in the snow on the north face of a huge mountain and are having a right old adventure. We reached our highest summit (1858m) along a knife-edge ridge caked in snow, but only at our third attempt. Found any pimples to climb? And how's the tan coming on?
Ben

The cliff-edged Archduke's Path.

The island's highest walkable point – the summit of Massanella.

Pick a perfect picnic spot...

**POSTCARD**

Ben,

A truly great day on Mallorca's highest accessible peak. Only the spiky grass kept us out of shorts and we had views across the whole island. Then it was back to the digs for cervezas on the terrace. The island's overrun with merry monks and possibly naughty nuns. Oh our aching limbs!

Guy

# The second 24 hours... (MALLORCA)

Now we've got the measure of what's on offer, and mindful of what we'd be doing were we in the UK, we're keen to bag a big summit. Massanella, the highest walkable peak on the island, is a natural choice.

Rising as if from a jungle in Borneo, our English guidebook informs us that a long walk up to a pass on its right side leads to a stiff, sustained scramble to the summit. It's a singularly sculpted mountain – steep, smooth sides with a crown of limestone forming an extensive summit. It looks like a lime jelly with a Viennetta balanced on top.

Guidebook time is 5 hours, plus whatever we spend fretting on the scramble. Once again the weather is from another season – a soft heat with cool breezes every now and again to soothe our brows.

The trail is easy to follow – the path marking system (red blobs of paint on rocks) makes it feel rather as if you're tracking a wounded fugitive, but it's surprisingly sure. Out of the forest I apply an appropriately exorbitant British measure of suncream until I'm as oily as something recently slipped into a wok, and in no danger of getting a tan. Up above us the crag is starting to assume greater dimensions and look as we might, there's no obvious line up it.

Many paths in these hills were made by the diggers of snowpits – deep, bus-sized holes used as a means of refrigeration for enervated Mallorcans in summer. The steep zigzags up to the pass (the Coll des Prat) hoist a view behind us – more pale Tryfans and cliffs ramping up from the forest. None of these mountains has been near a glacier and they appear ragged, almost playful, as a result, obeying only a few of the British rules about how mountains look.

The scramble is upon us. Our Cicerone guidebook understates its difficulties splendidly. The rock is grippy, but the crag has a kind of bulge which occasionally feels like it's prodding you out into open space.

We reach a middle band, a kind of balcony, and traverse round to the right. Eventually, the rock above looks pregnable, with two clear routes to the summit plateau. We're about to embark on one when a group of German walkers sweeps past us to start on the other. Germans are the most numerous of visitors to Mallorca, and exude at times an almost proprietorial air. But then even in pretty Valldemossa, many cafés advertise *frühstück* rather than *desayuno* at breakfast time. "This way!" one man says. "No, we're fine here," we answer. "This way!" he perseveres. He's still shaking his head when we meet him at the summit.

Here, from a reclining position on a warm sunbed of rock, you can view the whole island. Small terracotta-coloured towns seen from this angle stand out like cardboard Roman city models. The bay of Pollenca curves away with geometric precision, while closer at hand the cream limestone scenery is reminiscent of nothing so much as a Munro-sized Malham.

How frigid would the summit of Ben Nevis – the height we're at – be today, even assuming we could get to it? Already acclimatised to summer I shudder at the thought, as a few lightweight birds from the tit family bounce about the summit, with unfamiliar colours like a foreign air force. I quickly calculate the cost of the trip in my head, and reckon this top alone offsets it.

Descent over the other side is easier, the only hazard being the island's robust heather equivalent – plunge a hand into a clump and it yields about as much as coral. Plunging into the forest however is a relief – all that bitter, driving sun. How I feel for the chaps in Italy.

In the forest we bump into Zoë. Extending the customary timid "Ola" to the smiling stranger, it turns out this Keswick stage manager is a first-time visitor too. "I've never even flown before" she says. Zoë's staying in the village of Lluc: "The flights were £80 return and the monastery I'm staying in is £13 a night for a double ensuite, plus there's a bar ...". This island gets better and better.

Leaving the summit ridge of Pania della Croce, reluctantly...

It's bye for now to the scrambled edge of Massanella.

# Arrivederci, Italy

As we touched down in Britain, the animal carcasses were still burning and thousands of people were suffering the alarming symptoms of indoor fever. But we were safe, immunised by the exhaustion of a cappuccino comedown and the many, many metres of up, down and around that had kept our legs moving and our minds sane.

It had only cost four days and less than £250 each, so we'd neither broken the bank nor generated letters from the folk in personnel – not bad given I'd otherwise have a new telly by now, have forked out for cable and taken time off work just to get fat and depressed.

But perhaps best of all is that I now know a new mountain range. I have another group of hilly friends to welcome me with inclines and peaks the next time our own fair land goes belly up. It's my insurance policy, my little something for a rainy day, only there's no limit to my claims and this is one stash that can't be diminished. Just to prove it, I've booked my return flights, added

'helicopter' to my Italian vocabulary and 'Amazing!' to my English one, and worked out a route of red dotted lines. And this time, in case I'm wrong about God and the weather, I've already started praying...

# Adios, Mallorca

There's no substitute for having free access to the hills of home. But nor is there anything like a dash of something unfamiliar to spice up your walking life. So whether you leave the country under pressure of plague or just because you can, you can't lose by coming to Mallorca.

The seven million people who annually ply the beaches have pushed down the prices on the airlines; accommodation even in the better half of the island is cheap and plentiful; the walking is familiar, well waymarked and as exciting as you want to make it; and the weather in spring and autumn is the climatic promised land (average temperature 20°C and six hours of sunshine).

There are 33 walks in the Cicerone book graded for difficulty at B+ or above, and 40 others that'll do for the morning before your flight back. We had just scratched the surface of the island, but it had marked us pretty deeply. For an early taste of the summer walking that is slowly coming our way, Mallorca was brilliant – as a pressure release valve for caged Brits seeking escapist mountain thrills during a time of national crisis, it deserves to get an OBE.

# Fact file

## ITALY ▮▮

If you fancy a pizza da action this weekend, consider this...

**The Alpi Apu*whate*?** Apuane. Or, if you want it in English, the Apuan Alps.

**Never heard of them.** No, neither had we. But they're bang on the Med, just north of Pisa and within paint-flicking distance of Florence.

**So they're full of artists, are they?** Not quite, but they have provided marble for many of the world's finest works of art. So famous is the purity and texture of Apuan marble that it's been quarried for centuries and used by the likes of Michelangelo.

**So the hills have been ruined for walkers, then?** Far from it. Many people find a certain beauty in the quarries and the mountains are too big to be ruined by chipping of a few chisels.

**Sounds like I'm being conned...** Don't you believe it! You've got razor-sharp ridges everywhere you look, mountains up to almost 2000m and a network of *rifugios* (shelters) to take the sting out of camping. Which you're not allowed to do, by the way.

**And if I want to go right now?**

Then get packed and get on a plane, but make sure you take your crampons and ice axe – the range receives plenty

Illustrations by Jeremy Ashcroft

of snow. And if you intend to overnight in the hills, take a sleeping bag and stove for the winter bivouac shelters.

**Getting there** We flew to Bologna with a budget airline. From Bologna we hired a car with Holiday Autos.

**Where to stay** In Levigliani the Hotel Raffaello does a decent room with breakfast and can be contacted on – tel.

(00 39) 0584 778063 or booked through the English-speaking tourist office – tel. (00 39) 0584 48881. In the mountains Rifugio del Freo provided fine food and bunks for not too many lira, and the Rifugio Rossi alla Pania had a winter bivouac shelter. *Rifugios* are open weekends throughout the year and all week long during the summer months. Details from the Italian Alpine Club

web site – www.cai-svi.it

**What we did** From Levigliani we climbed Monte Corchia (1676m) and Pania della Croche (1858m) via paths 9, 122, 125, 7 and 126, plus a night each at Rifugio del Freo and Rifugio Rossi alla Pania. We had planned to follow the sharp scrambly ridge Uomo Morto to Pania Secca, but were turned back by the weather.

**Total ascent** 1600m

**Total distance** 14km

**Maps and guides** *Walking in Italy*, pb Lonely Planet offers a couple of suggestions for routes in the mountains.

Be warned that the Italian maps are awful and the 1:25,000 Edizione Multigraphic Parco delle alpi Apuane 101/102 only has contours at 25m intervals. Nonetheless, it's the best available and can be ordered from Stanfords or bought in local towns.

---

## MALLORCA ▤

Take two minutes to change your mind about Mallorca...

**Isn't it full of tourists?**

Actually, no. The beach and booze crowd

restrict themselves to the south side of the island. The mountainous north couldn't be more different.

**But it's a desert, right?** Wrong! Mallorca enjoys a warm climate but in spring it's still green and the temperature pleasant. Expect average temperatures of up to 20

degrees C in late spring and autumn.

**What about the hills?** The island has one big range containing about as many peaks as the Lake District but looking more like the limestone dales, in a bigger, more jagged way.

**Why should I care?** Because with short flying times and frequent departures you really can watch the drizzle from your work window on one day and be on warm, sunny fells by next morning.

**How much hassle will it be?** Minimal. Book a car and flights on the Internet, fly from an efficient regional airport, and it's less than an hour's drive from Palma airport to the mountains.

**Getting there** Cheap flights on the internet are best for short breaks – or for a week's stay you can sometimes ace it with a last-minute charter flight seat.

**Where to stay** There are plenty of hotels in the main mountain town of Soller. They come in six grades of price, denoted by square blue signs with a code letter. In ascending order of price they are: F for Fonda, CH for casa de huéspedes, P for Pension, Hs for Hostal, HsR for Hostal-residencia and H for Hotel.

Many walkers favour the cheap, eccentric monastery accommodation – bookable through local tourist offices or direct via the contacts on www.mallorcanow.com. Or try Lluc monastery, handy for Massanella – tel. (0034) 971 871525.

If you want to stay longer, we recommend ex-pat of 25 years Chris Goode, who lets an idyllic studio in the village of Valldemossa. Ideal for a walking couple, the studio costs £175-£240 a week and comes with excellent facilities – tel. (0034) 971 612197.

## Where we went
### The Archduke's Path
moderate

**Start** Valldemossa
**Distance** 16km
**Total ascent** 790m
**Time** 6 hours

### Massanella by the Coll des Prat hard

**Start** Lluc petrol station
**Distance** 12km
**Total ascent** 795m
**Time** 5½ hours

**Maps and guides** *The Cicerone Guide* by June Parker (ISBN 1 85284 250 4) is the best source of routes, but also check out *The Rough Guide*, by Phil Lee (ISBN 1 85828 165 2) and *Cordee's Mallorca*, by Rold Goetz (ISBN 3 7633 4805 0).

Maps of the island are little better than drawings, and the guidebooks' sketches are usually more useful. For the purposes of orientation, get the Freytag and Berndt 1:50,000 Mallorca Tramuntana, which covers all the best walking. Available from Stanfords.

Whoops – we missed
the ski-lift! Near the
Refuge de la Glère.

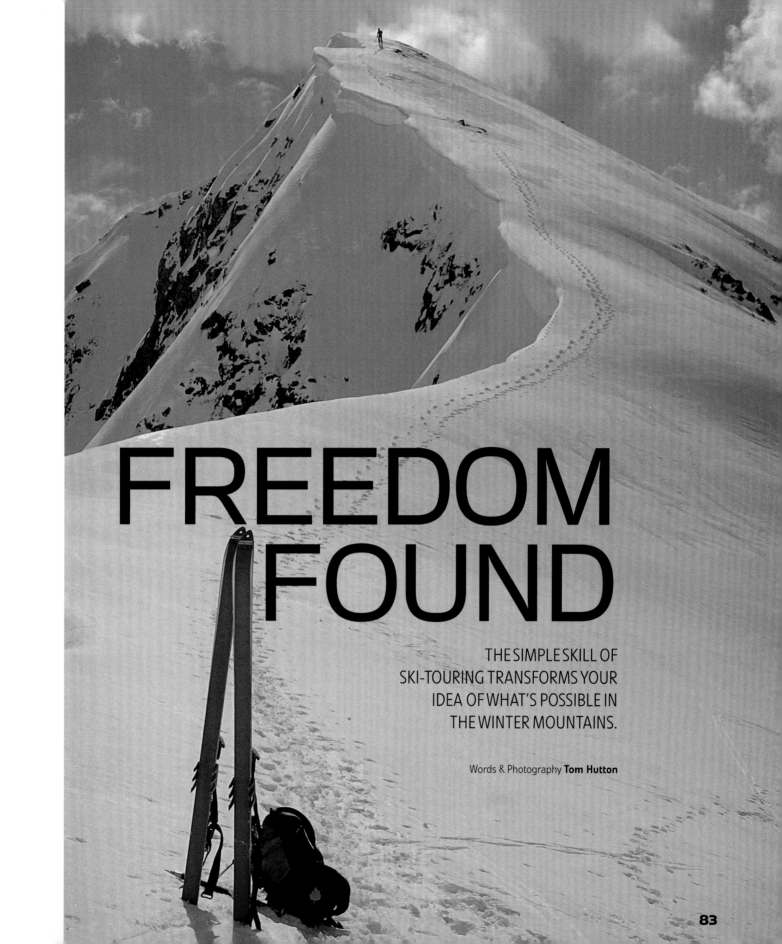

# FREEDOM FOUND

THE SIMPLE SKILL OF
SKI-TOURING TRANSFORMS YOUR
IDEA OF WHAT'S POSSIBLE IN
THE WINTER MOUNTAINS.

Words & Photography **Tom Hutton**

Turning on the style for a quick way down.

On the up in the Pas de la Crabe.

The end of another day. The lifts had stopped running and the pistes were empty. My skis glided silently over powdery snow. I paused to catch my breath and looked around.

In every direction, as far as the eye could see, there were mountains – tall, jagged peaks; magnificent rounded summits and dramatic rocky ridges. In the lengthening shadows, beneath one particularly spectacular rock face, I noticed a weak glimmer of light. I gazed harder and realised that it came from a small *refuge*, high up on the mountainside. At that moment, there was nowhere on earth I would rather have been.

Later, down in the village, the vision refused to subside and I found myself staring out at the darkened slopes, wondering what it would be like to be among them, to get away from the lifts and the pistes and the crowds, to really experience the freedom of the mountains.

One year later, with the image of the refuge still etched in my mind, I decided to find out. I booked my place on an 'Introduction to Ski-Touring' course with Pyrenean Mountain Tours, a British-run company, based in the small French Pyrenean town of Luz St Saveur. A few weeks later, with more than a little apprehension, I was sitting in the cosy bar of the Hotel des Cimes, perusing a well-prepared itinerary and supping on a cool beer.

The first lesson in ski-touring is about gear. Touring boots are like a cross between traditional ski boots and mountaineering boots. Clamp them tight and they hold your foot solid; turn a switch at the back and you can walk in them. In order to keep them light, they're not as high or as supportive as traditional ski boots – so they feel quite different to begin with.

The skis also take some getting used to. Again, in order to keep the weight down, they're lighter and generally more flexible than downhill skis. If you have downhill skied, it's common to go for a pair 20cm or so shorter than you'd normally use, although on your first day you spend most time skiing on-piste, just getting used to the feel of it all.

The crucial difference of course is the skiing uphill bit. We began day two by learning about avalanche transceivers and spent a while practising with them, buried in the snow. Once we'd got up to speed with this essential discipline, Simon, a partner in the company and someone passionate about all forms of ski-mountaineering, demonstrated the transformations necessary to

start climbing. Firstly, you disconnect the heel of the binding so your foot is hinged at the toe; secondly, you apply 'skins' to the skis. Again, it was all much simpler than I'd imagined; and within minutes we were all plodding uphill on our first mini-tour. The climb only lasted about an hour yet we were rewarded with some stunning views as we crested the narrow ridge.

The ski down was tremendous, starting steep on untracked spring snow; we funnelled down into a wooded valley and traversed back to the car park.

At this stage, I'd already learned enough to know that there are a lot of misconceptions about ski-touring. First and by far the biggest is that it's an elite sport, only available to expert skiers. The touring season usually starts towards the end of the alpine season and, as the slopes get warmer and the weather more predictable, the skiing becomes easier. While there's still a small chance of fresh snow, the majority of touring takes place on spring snow, which is usually fairly firm and even smoother than a piste. For this course, the ability to ski a typical red run, in control and with linked turns, was the only prerequisite.

The second popular misconception is that the climbing is only for the extremely fit. A good guide will always choose the easiest way up the mountain and, in many ways, it's easier than walking; your feet literally glide across the snow, often following in the tracks of others. Any reasonably fit hill-walker would cope admirably on this type of tour.

With the preliminaries out of the way, it was time to undertake a more serious adventure. Simon gave way to Richard, a local mountain guide, for a one-day tour to the Col d'Oncet. The route was perfect for our level; climbing steadily beside a stream for some distance before a short steep section gained the top. It was a glorious day and although the sun was beating down on us for most of the way, there were smiles all round as we heaved ourselves onto the top.

Leaving the skis and bags at the col, we climbed the final 100m on foot. This is where touring comes into its own. Not only do you have the high of reaching the summit but you also have the anticipation of a long, off-piste ski back down. This one didn't disappoint at all and, all too soon, we found ourselves back on the road waiting for a lift back to Luz.

The one-day tour had been a real success and, by now, both my confidence and my skiing had come on considerably. I now felt

Refuge de la Glare – a hillbound hideaway.

ready for the main event: a three-day tour around the Refuge de la Glère in the Pyrenees National Park. Although the standard of skiing in the group was pretty even, it had become clear, over the week, that there was a difference in the speed at which people wanted to climb and ski. This is quite common, and a second guide allowed us to split into even smaller groups. We set out from the resort of La Mongie and, after using a couple of chairlifts to gain some initial height, we broke away from the piste to climb over the Pas de la Crabe.

This was an experience that I won't forget in a hurry. To get into the adjoining valley we had to squeeze through a chest-high, shoulder-width crack in a steep rock face. One by one, we passed our skis through to Richard and scrambled through. Emerging into bright sunshine, we skied safely down into the valley then stopped to attach skins before starting on a long climb over the next ridge. An airy traverse took us onto a narrow shoulder where we stopped for a bite to eat, and a gape at the stupendous view.

Another fun descent, followed by a short climb, took us to the lake beneath the refuge. I found a bunk, sorted out a few bits and pieces, and then climbed up high onto the ridge to watch the sunset. These were magical moments – alone and surrounded by some of the most magnificent scenery on earth. Only cold and hunger eventually persuaded me to climb back down for some dinner. I went to bed early; I was going to need all my strength for the ascent of the Turon de Neouvielle.

We rose early and set off in the dark. With little in the way of shade, it was important to get most of the hard work out of the way before the sun got too hot. With both skins and *Harscheissen* (ski crampons) fitted, we pressed on relentlessly, stopping only occasionally for food or water. Though I'd been in the area for a few days now, I still couldn't stop gazing around in sheer wonderment at the spectacle of the landscape; and it was even better knowing that we had it all to ourselves. A fleeing ptarmigan broke my stride for a few moments but, other than that, I was keeping a fine

All this effort will soon pay off!

rhythm and hardly noticed the climb at all.

Everything had gone according to plan and, after only a few hours, we reached the foot of a steep, narrow gully; still mercifully shaded from the worst of the sun. This was to be the toughest part of the whole climb and it seemed like an eternity before, panting wildly, I pulled myself out onto the flatter ground above.

Thankfully, from here, the final leg to the 3025m summit was nothing more than a steady rising traverse. It felt good knowing that I'd climbed over a thousand metres before lunch. It felt even better, knowing that I was going to be skiing back down the same distance straight after.

We whiled away a pleasant hour or so on the summit, eating lunch and admiring the views. Eventually, we removed skins, clamped down boots, and set off down the mountain for an hour and a half of ski heaven. After negotiating a couloir that tested my ability to the limit, the slope eased to an almost perfect angle – steep enough to be fun, not so steep as to be life-threatening. For a good way down, the surface was covered by 10cm of windblown powder – without doubt, the most exhilarating skiing I'd ever experienced.

For the last day of the tour, we chose to climb Mont Arrouy, a nearby peak a few hundred metres lower than yesterday's triumph but every bit as spectacular. Somehow, we all managed to cram onto the slender summit ridge and, after a brief drink, set off on the final descent of the week. With my confidence at an all-time high, I've never enjoyed skiing so much and was even leaving perfectly spaced tracks, snaking down the mountain behind me (I think they were mine anyway...). We eventually reached the snowline at the bottom of the valley and prepared for a final walk-out.

Six days earlier, ski-touring had been something of a mystery to me. In one short week, somewhere on the snow-covered slopes of the Pyrenees, my apprehension had turned into addiction. There is no real mystery to ski-touring. It is, quite simply, a lifetime pass to the true freedom of the mountains.

# BELLISSIMO!

TO HELL WITH ENGLISH RESERVE – WE'RE GOING
OUT ON A LIMB HERE AND SAYING THE VIA
FERRATAS IN ITALY'S DOLOMITES ARE THE BEST
MOUNTAIN FUN IN THE WORLD... EVER!

Words **Guy Procter** Photography **Tom Bailey**

*'Till within the last six or eight years the Dolomite district
was scarcely known even by name to any but scientific
travellers. Even now, the general public is so slightly
informed upon the subject that it is by no means
uncommon to find educated persons who have never
heard of the Dolomites at all, or who take them for a
religious sect, like the Mormons or the Druses.'*
**Amelia B. Edwards, Untrodden Peaks and
Unfrequented Valleys, 1873**

Big up the Sella mountain massif! The top of the Pisciadù via ferrata.

Half an hour from the car, on the Cirspitze ridge above the Gardena Pass.

Your mission for today is to find among your friends and relations those who have been to the Dolomites – and throttle them. Because they, and their like, have been sitting on a rather large secret for over a hundred years.

You know that paranoid feeling you get after watching a Channel Four documentary in which it is revealed every thousandth person you pass in the street is a serial killer, every hundredth a psychopath, every tenth someone who bought *Millennium Prayer* by Sir Cliff Richard? Just when you thought you knew about the world, a new and sinister sub-plot has you looking out of the corner of your eye. That's how I felt when I came back from the Dolomites. Why, why, WHY hadn't someone told me about this wonderful place before?

So, the dry facts: they're in northern Italy, a more temperate tail-end of the Alps, roughly 60 by 60 miles in extent. Among them 18 peaks top 10,000ft, the highest being the Marmolada (10,964ft), whose 2,000ft south wall represents the most famous view – at sunset it lights up like a pink, orange and crimson cinema screen. They were named for a geologist called Dieudonné Dolomieu, who described the unique limestone of which they are formed, and most of the main summits were bagged (by Brits, as it happens) in the 1860s and 70s.

In real time, coming to the Dolomites is a blur of expectations flouted, senses supercharged and wild, childish hopes fulfilled. First, forget what you thought about what mountains looked like. I thought I had the phenomenon of mountain formation pretty well sussed, in a GCSE geo-cookery kind of way. Pre-heat the world to the correct temperature. Take two tectonic plates; combine. Your mixture will now rise to form lots of volcanoes. Let these cool. Next, neaten any sharp edges with a glacier or two. Finally, allow to weather for millions and millions of years.

But the Dolomites' grotesque spires appear to owe nothing to the normal ideas of geological decorum or even gravity. Their outlines don't relate to what I understand about how the world is. Unlike many more traditionally 'Alpine' destinations, here the bits of the mountain you actually want to get to tend to start straight from the road, not 5,000ft up, beyond forested nursery slopes plied by overpriced cablecars.

What does one DO in these outlandish mountains? Luckily, an activity has evolved that's almost as distinctive as the venue. It's called Doing the Via Ferrata, and it's better than sliced bread.

*'For those who love mountain-climbing and mountain air, and who desire when they travel to leave London and Paris behind them, the Dolomites offer a 'playground' far more attractive than the Alps.'*

Via ferrata literally means 'iron way', and it denotes the cables which have been lashed across many of the most spectacular mountains. The point? Well, when the first were fixed in the dying days of the 19th century it was to make tricky sections of mountaineering routes easier.

Then in World War One, the Italian army laid a whole lot more to assist their eccentric assault on the Austrians (mostly involving bombing crags so they fell on the opposition). After the war, the routes were turned over to climbers to use, but it wasn't until the 1930s that via ferrata-building entered its next phase. The SAT mountaineering club (Societá Alpinistica Trentina) together with the CAI (Club Alpino Italiano) installed dozens more, with the aim of shortening and easing access to popular 'real' climbing grounds.

But the cables were coming into their own; after World War Two, the Bochette Way was completed – one of the first long via ferratas, and one which really crystallised their distinct appeal as linear adventures in themselves, rather than mere approach routes or summit-seeking problem-solvers. The door to the rarefied pleasures and extreme situations of mountaineers and rock-climbers was laid open.

*'That a certain amount of activity and some power to resist fatigue, are necessary to the proper enjoyment of this new playground, must be conceded from the beginning.'*

Today there are over 80 routes, from simple scrambles where the cable's only needed for protection, to really exposed climbs where you'll find yourself hauling up on it. Most routes take two to three hours in ascent, with an easier walk-off. There is no universal consensus on grading, but local guides use a simple system of A to G – A being easy-peasy and G being long, remote and technically challenging climbing.

We had arrived in Corvara, a small western town, in the dark. Like the Christmas Coca-Cola advert, the settlement twinkled in a hollow at the foot of a windy road. All around, mountains rose, and the moon lit them tantalisingly. We couldn't wait for daylight to come round.

With only two days to savour the region, we were keen to get into the thick of things. Over breakfast we discussed plans with our guide. Antonia, a New Zealander with our hosts Collett's Mountain Holidays and several seasons on the via ferratas and winters on the neighbouring pistes under her belt, inspired us with confidence and enthusiasm. Our climbing abilities were mixed, and we really wanted to know that we weren't going to be made to cry – in front of a girl. "You'll be right," she asserted, with her country's trademark 'anything's possible, or at least nothing's gone wrong yet' gung-ho. It was infectious.

She reeled off names, and I tried to keep up with the one English guidebook there is until my thumb got hot. "Pisciadù!" she'd said with finality. I found the page as we pulled out onto the road.

*'The Pisciadù Path, a monument of climbing-path building-art,*

Through an early morning haze, Antonia pointed to a tiny filament laid across a fearsome gorge. Then she said: "You'll be crossing that later."

Hard to believe this lot is accessible to UK hill-walkers with no special skills other than a head for heights... but it is.

Sassolungo (below) is the site of some great Grade E via ferratas; on the left Ben gears up for a short, sharp scramble to the Pizes de Cirspitze; Haus Valentin (bottom right) is a guest house run in summer by Collett's Mountain Holidays and where we stayed. It's typical of the region's hospitable character.

Ladders, Our Lady and lots and lots of clear blue sky – you could get used to this.

The Gothic slab-sides of the Gruppo Sella (below) don't seem to owe much to the laws of gravity – but they're not impregnable. Just look for the red crossed dotted lines on your map.

Signs (below) are all bilingual – the Dolomites used to be part of Austria before World War One, and there are still plenty of German speakers around. Some are trilingual, with Ladin, the local dialect which has evolved into a discrete language, featuring too; the government has pumped money into the area in the form of generous grants, to keep any potential nationalist tensions firmly buried under prosperity.

*offers with its calculated measure of technical perfection the greatest degree of unalloyed enjoyment of rock.' Höfler/Werner, Klettersteigführer Dolomiten (Via Ferrata – Scrambles in the Dolomites), 1982.*

Our route had a ringing endorsement from the German judges then, albeit slightly unhinged. I soon felt sick reading the route description, snatching words and phrases like 'excitingly beautiful' and 'really exposed' before the car lurched at that velocity known as 'local speed' round hairpin after hairpin.

The climb is a Grade D (a suitable starting level for confirmed scramblers), good for three hours of ascent and two hours down. It starts innocuously enough with a gentle forest walk, the only obstacle a ladder up and over a drum of steep rock. Ladders like this, and their cool, clammy rungs, are one of the most characteristic features in the Dolomites. Some have each rung stapled to the rock individually, others are more like discarded window cleaners' ladders.

Eventually the walking ends and then, unemphatically, you're on the via ferrata.

It's the same blind urge to climb you get at the foot of a branchy tree. There's something about combining feet and hand movements which puts you in a purposeful trance. The views, as you can see, are stunning, but the instant pleasure is in the stabbing of feet into rock pockets, the snicking of hands into rough holds just the right distance away, and creeping into greater and greater attics of exposure.

*'For ladies, side-saddles are absolutely necessary, there being only two in the whole country, and but one of these for hire.' (Untrodden Peaks and Unfrequented Valleys).*

The gear, attached to the rock and attached to you, is what frees you to enjoy the experience so much. All you need is a climbing harness, and some rope, divided into two arm-lengths by a 'kinetic friction device' – basically a brake – each with a karabiner at the end. One karabiner links you to the wire rope, and the other waits, clipped to your harness, for when you have to leapfrog a joint where the wire is fastened to the rock. It's a painless process, repeated a hundred or more times in a day, and it's at these changeovers you get a chance to soak up the views.

By about the fortieth clip-unclip we had reached – seemingly effortlessly – a dizzying altitude, and the steepness of the slopes below made you feel every foot. Photographer Tom dropped a lens cover and it tumbled for some long seconds before it went out of sight, still miles above the ground. Yet despite this demonstration of gravitational consequences, here we were, lolling on the wire in perfect serenity. I wouldn't have credited my brain with such coolness before the climb, but it just goes to show what a sense of security does for you.

Ahead, lofty dolomitic towers – hardly diminished by two hours' climbing – reared like moon-mountains; below, between our feet, the tops of pine trees stood like pipe cleaners in the baize of Alpine pastures. In between was a vast gulf of blue sky and air – via ferrata country.

The climbing eased, and we had lunch sitting on a grassy shelf – at other times it would have seemed a risky perch, but now we were as comfortable with exposure as birds.

Who'd have thought you could be happy with exposure like this? One of the Pisciadù path's more vertiginous sections.

The rough, snaggly rock was perfect for the final stretch of scrambling (we'd determined to try not to use the wire to haul ourselves up), as the route contorted around sub-summits which projected out into the void on the other side of the massif.

All that stood between us and an easy walk to the *rifugio* which marked the end of the Pisciadù path was a tiny via ferrata bridge. Made of thin slats seemingly supported by coat-hangers and the power of prayer, you'd have thought twice about using it to cross a beck. This being the Dolomites, it actually spanned a freakish cleft in the mountain – a yawning chasm of death thousands of feet deep. Imagine Striding Edge with a crevasse half way along which went down to Red Tarn. Clipping into the wire, and taking my place like a cut-price Indiana Jones at the bridge's edge, I wondered if real life would ever again appear quite so like a Road Runner cartoon. Walking on tip-toe so as to be lighter, I crossed the rippling bridge without plunging to my doom.

Rifugios – stonking great cafés right in the loft-space of the mountains – are one thing the Dolomites share with the rest of the Alps. Unlike, say, the Snowdon café, whose array of warmed-over microwave snacks is liable to make you want to throw yourself from the nearest cliff, the rifugio is a haven of good food, good feeling and civilisation. At least, so I felt after a plate of chef-cooked bolognese and a bottle of Nastro Azzurro. Sitting overlooking the bleached-denim coloured lake below the rifugio, a cool, glacial breeze drying our foreheads, a forkful of good food hovering between plate and lip, and a size XXL scramble under our belts (and our fingernails), I had never before felt more completely satisfied by a mountain day.

On the last day we took the forecast like addicts: a good morning, possible afternoon storms. If we wanted to go climbing lightning conductors, the a.m. had a definite edge.

To the Pizes de Cirspitze we went this time – a quick Grade C from the very top of the Gardena pass, and our farewell to the Dolomites – for now. This time the approach was through Alpine meadows, studded by chunky wooden shepherds' huts. The sun was white and piercing as we topped the grassy tongue and arrived at the foot of a long wall of crags, spurs and buttresses. Our route was a thousand feet high – a concentrated scramble so convoluted and with so many good juggy holds, we gobbled it in what seemed like minutes.

The summit just had room for three to sit around, the ground plunging away toward sylvan meadows and deep valleys either side. A metal cross sprang from its very apex, making us feel we were sitting atop Lincoln Cathedral – and I for one was beaming with all the guileless glee of a convert.

Back in the valleys, the positive reinforcement would be relentless. With via ferratas being so accessible, there's none of that hard-core competitive atmosphere you can get in some Alpine venues. And the beer's about half the price it is in, say, Chamonix. The people, a trilingual compôte of Italian, Austrian and Ladin, are friendly. In fact, if you sense I'm struggling to find anything bad to say, and even to finish the story, you're right – sorry to leave you hanging, but there's something about a visit to the Dolomites you just don't want to... end.

# FACT FILE

## WHEN TO GO

Late June to late September are the extremes for comfortable via ferrataing. If you want to make sure all the rifugios and lifts are open and there's no snow on the ground, wait until July to start. Some of the most popular routes (like Pisciadù) can get busy, especially in August, when Italy has its own mass holiday.

## GETTING THERE

Venice's airport, Treviso, is the nearest touchdown. The cheapest fares are on the internet – www.ryanair.com. Or phone – tel. (0870) 1569569.

Driving on to the Dolomites (it's best to hire a car) takes about three hours; make sure you get some low-denomination currency at the airport for the two or three road tolls on the way.

## MAKING IT EASY

We put our arrangements (apart from flights) in the hands of UK-based Dolomites specialist Collett's Mountain

Holidays. They offer car hire from the airport, village accommodation in well-situated Arabba or Pedraces, and the services of enthusiastic via ferrata experts, who can advise you where to go. They also lead via ferrata walks five days a week. Collett's – tel. (01763) 289660/ 289680; fax (01763) 289690 or email admin@colletts.co.uk; also try Marmot Trails – tel. (020) 8461 5516.

## WHERE TO STAY

If you want to go it alone, there is plenty of accommodation, thanks to the ski crowds who pitch up in winter. Cortina is the biggest tourist centre, but all Dolomite towns are equally well sited for those who fancy via ferrata action.

The Italian Tourist Office in London will give you accommodation lists – tel. (020) 7408 1254. Or try the Dolomites' own promotional website – www.dolomiti.it

## VIA FERRATA SAFETY

● You don't need to be a rock-climber, but you should be a capable scrambler.

● Exposure comes quickly and easily on many routes, and the last thing you want is to 'freeze' halfway up. If Crib Goch doesn't worry you, these shouldn't, but test the water on easy grades first if in doubt.

● The going may be fun and straightforward, but these are still the Alps, and you should be aware of the hazards weather and altitude can present. Get the BMC's pamphlet on Alpine conditions if you're a first-time visitor – tel. (0161) 445 4747.

● Lightning and iron cables, er, don't mix. Forecast-checking is therefore a must – available where you stay.

## DOLOMITES WEBSITES

**Official site:** www.piuitalia2000.it
**Local site:** www.dolomiti.it
**Personal site:** http://freespace.virgin.net/paul.benham/dolo/intro.html

## TOURIST INFORMATION

**London** – Italian Tourist Office in London – tel. (020) 7408 1254.
**Corvara** – tel. (0039) 0471 836176; – fax. (0039) 0471-836540
**Pedraces** – tel. 0039 0471 839695; – fax. (0039) 0471 839573

---

# GEAR

● **Clothing** – UK hill-walking waterproofs and warmwear are fine for the conditions, but they must not interfere with your harness.

● **Boots** – in summer, UK 3-4 season boots are fine, preferably ones that give you some 'feel' to aid the climbing. Scarpa's El Caps (£135) are pretty unbeatable if you're feeling flush.

● **Harness** – a climbing harness such as you would use on any UK climbing wall is fine. A full-body harness can give you extra confidence, even if it looks, as you can see (right), a bit noddy.

● **Specialised gear** – traditional 'cowtail' arrangements take a length of rope with a friction device in the middle attached to your harness loop. With a karabiner clipped into a loop at each end of the rope, you're ready to go. The nub of it is the friction device – if you fall it absorbs the sudden impact by letting the length of the cowtail slide through slowly.

Best of all is Petzl's modern version of the cowtail – the Zyper-Y, which costs £27. Stockist details – tel. (015396) 25493.

● **Gloves** – avoid blisters and 'hot hands' with some grippy-palmed gloves – The leather-palm North Face Guide Gloves (£45) are an ideal choice.

● **Helmet** – bit of a no-brainer.

● **Maps** – the Tabacco series (1:25,000) is accurate and beautiful to look at. Buy locally or order from Stanfords in London – tel. (020) 7836 2260.

---

# TECHNIQUE

**1** Clip in – making sure your rope isn't twisted

**2** **Use your feet** – same as any climbing, you'll go further and tire slower if you use leg power to push yourself up, rather than hauling on your arms

**3** **Change over** – When you get to an anchor point, clip your second karabiner onto the new section of wire. Then (and only then!) unclip your original krab

**4** **Slide up** – keep your cowtail hooked over your arm to keep your karabiner sliding easily up the wire

**5** **Keep scoffing** – with your brain, arms and legs absorbed in action, you won't feel particularly tired. But rest assured, you're burning calories

**6** **Keep looking** – the wire feels safe, but you need to check the safety of each pitch just as you would in free climbing – as well as applying your usual mountain sense to the conditions

# ANIMAL MAGIC

GLACIER NATIONAL PARK IS A TREASURE TROVE OF PRISTINE TRAILS GIVING YOU THE CHANCE TO GET UNCOMFORTABLY CLOSE TO NATURE. **ALF ALDERSON** GOES DOWN TO THE WOODS ARMED WITH LOCAL BEAR KNOW-HOW...

At up to seven feet long and 800lb or more in weight, a grizzly bear can peel a walker out of their Gore-Tex quicker than you can skin a banana. So when you're walking in the Rockies it pays to be 'bear aware'... and there's no end of people waiting to dish out advice.

Most of the folk who live around North America's Rocky Mountains have a stockpile of bear stories and are keen to tell you their method for avoiding a run-in with a grizzly. Unfortunately, when I finally stumbled across one, that advice wasn't to hand.

I was hiking along the 10-mile Iceberg Lake Trail on the eastern side of Glacier National Park, a relatively busy footpath named after the small bergs which float here in summer. The path passes up through huckleberry bushes, which are prime bear feeding territory, into shady, fragrant forest and across dazzlingly bright streams, with the blue-shadowed, serrated ridge of the massive Garden Wall arête bearing down on you from the west and marking the Continental Divide.

Yes, I'd heard a bundle of ursine anecdotes and I'd read a stack of bear-related literature before I set off on the walk. I'd noted the signs tacked to trees that warned of recent grizzly sightings in the vicinity. But when I saw four people some distance above the path waving at me and frantically pointing downhill, I couldn't work out why they were behaving in this idiotic fashion.

There had to be a reason for their manic and strangely silent gesticulations, but having grown up in a country where the adder is the most lethal predator, it took a while to realise it might be animal-related. Following the invisible line their fingers were stabbing towards, I finally saw it. Some 300 yards below me there was a fully-grown grizzly foraging for food.

All the advice I had been given melted away. I couldn't remember if I was supposed to run, play dead or sing at the top of my voice. All I could do was savour every moment of a unique mountain experience that is virtually impossible to repeat in Europe. Fortunately, the bear didn't spot me; and after a couple of minutes he ambled off into the bushes and was lost from sight. I had enough common sense to watch quietly.

And it didn't stop there. On the way back down to my car I saw another two black bears foraging through the bushes high up on the mountainside. Once again our encounter wasn't too close, which was a good job. The only piece of bear-encounter advice that came to me was a quote from Bill Bryson. He reckons the best defence in bear country is to 'hike with someone slower than yourself'. Not a lot of use for a solitary soul like myself!

It turned out that I had been exceptionally lucky to see these beautiful creatures. While several outdoor types I met in the Rockies had had some kind of bear experience, few had actually seen one that close up. Most of the tales I heard seemed to have happened to 'friends of

Cool evening light hits Glacier National Park.

friends'. There were plenty of people living on the edge of towns who'd had their trash cans rifled by black bears. Food is a good reason for bears to forsake the wilds of the Rockies and head into a more urban environment. As John Muir said, 'to a bear almost everything is food except granite'. And he wasn't wrong. One guy I met wandered into his garden one morning to find a fully grown grizzly batting a computer monitor around with his front paws before making a heroic attempt to digest this sumptuous cube of glass, plastic and silicon chip.

And then there was Rob, a friend from over the border in British Columbia, whose garden would be overrun with bears looking for something a little stronger. "Every fall, when the fruit's dropped off the trees, I catch the odd black bear rolling around drunk having snacked on the half-rotten, semi-fermented fruit. It's amusing to watch, but you certainly don't want to get on the wrong side of a half-cut grizzly," said Rob.

There are times when destiny throws you into a bear encounter, which is what happened to one ski instructor I met on the trail. "I was out on my mountain bike and came shooting round the bend on a forest road when I almost ran right into a bear," he explained. "We were both terrified and shot off in opposite directions, only to meet again on another bend a few hundred yards later and then tear along parallel to each other before the bear eventually crashed off into the trees. It was awesome!"

No-one I met, though, had been unlucky enough to experience a bear attack – indeed, friends living close to Glacier were somewhat miffed when I returned with my bear story. They'd lived there for over five years and had never seen one, but this Limey turns up and gets a front row seat within a few days...

Unfortunately there are no hard and fast rules as to what you should do if you come into closer contact with a bear than you might wish to. Even reading a definitive bear book such as *Backcountry Bear Basics* by expert Dave Smith, who has spent over 30 years living in grizzly country, you come away with the message that experts can't totally agree on the best way to deal with a bear encounter.

The essential advice when you're on the trail, however, is to make plenty of noise to warn bears of your presence and give them time to scarper, since the one thing that is agreed upon is that bears are no more eager to come into contact with humans than we are with them. Smith advises clapping and shouting "Hey, bear!" at intervals. He has little time for bear bells which attach to your rucksack and tinkle gently to warn of your approach. They're not that effective, and locals joke that the best way to recognise bear scat is to look for the stuff with bear bells in it.

It may seem strange to be wandering through the mountains creating a hullabaloo, but it's better than walking around a corner to encounter a startled grizzly. Everyone else will be probably be doing the same anyway: after all this is

What not to do when faced with a bear attack.

ALF ALDERSON

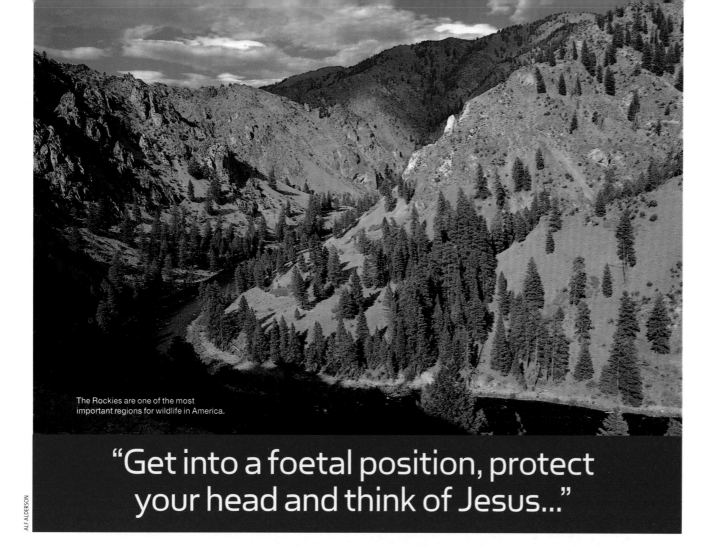

The Rockies are one of the most important regions for wildlife in America.

ALF ALDERSON

# "Get into a foetal position, protect your head and think of Jesus..."

America – home of the brave, and land of the free of inhibitions.

Useful advice is always easy to come by when you're on the trail too. When I was hiking in Glacier I met a ranger who informed me that it was better not to be out close to sundown. That's when bears start emerging from their dens, and it's not a good time to be walking alone. I was doing both and, looking back at our chat, I think this was him diplomatically telling me I was a butty short of Yogi and Boo-Boo's picnic basket.

The advice you do get runs utterly at odds with instinct. If you do meet a bear, Montana's Flathead National Forest advises that you don't leg it. I beg your pardon?! They might be as heavy as a small car, but they can easily outrun the fastest human. And don't think trees are going to offer you much sanctuary either. Do you really think you can get up that fir faster than a bear with a sore head?

You should stand your ground, avoid direct eye contact (which the bear will see as a threat) and – if the odds are in your favour and you haven't loaded your pockets with pungent bear snacks – there's a good chance it will simply look you over and amble off.

But there is always the chance of attack. The *Rough Guide to the Rockies* devotes two pages to dealing with just such an eventuality, titled "When things are truly grim…"

Playing dead is the generally accepted way of dealing with a grizzly attack. "Get into a foetal position, protect your head and think of Jesus*," says David Stanley, a bear expert from the Alaska-Yukon region. (*Non-Christians should feel free to insert the prophet, messiah or deity of their choice…)

With black bears, however, you're advised to fight back. Which is all very well as long as you're sure it's a black bear rather than a

grizzly which is bearing down on you – but how many people can distinguish between the two when face to face with several hundred pounds of angry bear meat? Dave Smith points out that if you fight back against a grizzly the severity of your injuries will usually be worse. But he adds laconically that if the attack lasts for more than a minute you will probably have to fight back to have any chance of surviving. So don't forget to set your stopwatch.

Having said all this, the one thing to keep in mind before you scare yourself witless about ever setting foot in the Rockies is that bears will not be lurking around every crag and fir tree waiting to pounce on you. And unless you're very unlucky or very foolish, the chances of being attacked are extremely slim.

And don't let yourself be psyched out by the locals' little mind games. One summer I was planning a hike up into the Bitterroot Mountains to overnight alone at the 6,000ft West Fork Butte lookout cabin, which is rented out by the Forestry Service. The night before I'd lodged at a delightful B&B in the nearby and very lovely Lochsa Valley. The owners, a gregarious couple of anglophiles called Ruth and Jim May, spent most of the evening I was there plying me with tales of neighbours' dogs and cats being taken by bears and mountain lions, and friends' close encounters with grizzlies, moose and other large, fierce creatures apparently jostling in the queue to have a set-to with a human.

"You do have a shotgun with you – doncha?" asked Jim, clearly trying to get a reaction. I was more than happy to oblige and started to quiz him feverishly on the likelihood of me becoming bear fodder. Even though he assured me the chances were slim, his conversation kept surfacing in my memory. I was hiking alone on

ALF ALDERSON

Above: the Middle Fork of the Salmon River.

empty trails high up, on my way to the isolated, unpopulated mountain range that sits astride Idaho and Montana. These are two of the remotest, least populated states in the USA.

The only thing that surprised me, considering the previous night's tales, was that I couldn't hear the wildlife crashing around in the trees as they tussled for a vantage point from which to ambush me. The only wild mammals I saw were a white-tailed deer and a few chipmunks… and that was enough to give me the willies. But to put things into perspective, there have been only 10 fatal bear attacks in Glacier National Park since it was established in 1910, which is an average of one per decade. Considering the fact that 1.73 million people visited the park last year, it seems bears are probably going out of their way to avoid humans.

Nevertheless, the fact that you might just come face to face with a bear adds a new and altogether more serious element to hiking

in the Rockies. After my experience in Glacier I cast aside the usual English reserve and followed the example of the locals on my ventures into the mountains in Montana and Idaho, singing, shouting and clapping as I made my way along the trails. I was also careful to ensure that any food and rubbish was stored well away from the campsite in airtight boxes and inaccessible locations, since bears have a phenomenal sense of smell.

The Rockies' upland landscape has barely changed since explorers Lewis and Clark first traversed the region 200 years ago, and creatures that are higher up the food chain than humans are as much a part of that landscape as its mountains, forests, rivers and lakes. While that makes a trip into the mountains more hazardous, it also takes you closer to nature in a way that's hard to replicate in Europe. As Dave Smith says: "If we can accommodate bears in our world, it will be a better place for us to live."

# Into the wild

The epic scale of North America's backcountry means that you could be walking in the company of some pretty impressive wildlife. But bears aren't the only 'ornery critters' you might encounter on the Stateside. And you might not need to use your binoculars...

## grizzly bear
### *Ursus arctos*

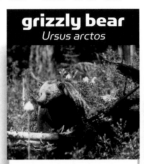

IDAHO FISH AND GAME

**Length** 2.1m

**Height at shoulder** 0.9-1.2m

**Average weight** 200-650kg

**Appearance** These large brown bears have a distinctive shoulder hump (extra muscle), long front claws and a long muzzle

**Distribution** In semi-open country in mountainous areas. Widely found in Canada, south of Alaska and from British Columbia to the Rockies

**How to avoid** Don't try to outrun, they can hit 35mph for short bursts. Instead, try shouting 'hey bear' and never get caught between a mother and her cubs. Don't fight back

**FEAR FACTOR 9**

## black bear
### *Ursus americanus*

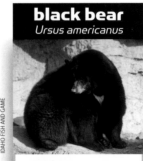

**Length** 1.5m

**Height at shoulder** 1.0-1.2m

**Average weight** 70-135kg

**Appearance** Darker than the average grizzly and lacking the distinctive shoulder hump

**Distribution** Alaska, Canada, USA to Mexico

**How to avoid** Make plenty of noise, keep food away from campsite. Never get caught between a mother and her cubs. Stay calm and avoid eye contact. Some people carry pepper spray with them

**FEAR FACTOR 7**

## elk
### *Cervus elephas*

**Height at shoulder** 1.5m

**Average weight** 315kg

**Appearance** Stag on steroids

**Distribution** They live in a variety of habitats from coastal forests to alpine meadows. Widely distributed across western North America. For most of the year cows and calves live in loose herds while bulls live in bachelor groups or alone

**How to avoid** There have been recorded attacks by female elks protecting their young. Never come between a mother and her calf

**FEAR FACTOR 3**

## mountain lion
### (cougar) *Puma concolor*

**Length** 120cm

**Height at shoulder** 76cm

**Average weight** 32-77kg

**Appearance** Large slender cat with noticeably long tail. Light tawny colour which can appear grey or black depending on light conditions

**Distribution** This has the widest distribution of any wild cat and can be found from North to South America. Very difficult to spot

**How to avoid** Mountain lions are expert stalkers. If you are attacked by one, make lots of noise, raise yourself up as big as possible and fight back

**FEAR FACTOR 6**

## grey wolf
### (timber wolf) *Canis lupus*

**Height at shoulder** 0.75m

**Average weight** 25-52kg

**Appearance** The ancestor of the domestic dog, grey wolves resemble German shepherds or huskies. They range in colour from grey or black to all white

**Distribution** 6-8,000 wolves in Alaska and 3,500 in six other states. Generally found in forests, tundra, deserts, plains or mountains

**How to avoid** Recorded wolf attacks on humans are very rare, but have been known when food is scarce

**FEAR FACTOR 5**

## moose *Alces alces*

**Height at shoulder** 2m

**Average weight** 500kg

**Appearance** Bulky body with a short tail and disproportionately large head. Long square muzzle with a 'bell' that hangs under the throat; this flap of skin grows up to 25cm on males and is used for communication and display

**Distribution** Alaska to the northern Rocky Mountains and eastward to Newfoundland

**How to avoid** Attacks are rare and most likely to occur if you come between a mother and calf. If you are charged, get behind a tree. If it attacks, get on the ground, lie still and cover your head

**FEAR FACTOR 3**

## Fact file
### GLACIER NATIONAL PARK
This is regarded as the most important biosphere reserve in the lower 48 states. It was designated a National Park in 1910, following a petition from Dr George Bird Grinnell to the government

### GETTING THERE
Fly to Salt Lake City then take an internal flight to either Idaho (Boise, Pocatello or Idaho Falls) or Montana (Bozeman, Billings, Missoula or Kalispell)

### WHEN TO HIKE
June to September. The rest of the year there's a risk of rain, snow and frost, especially up high

### MAPS
Most hikers use the US GS 1:24,000 series, or maps from Earthwalk Press and Trails Illustrated. Rand McNally's *Central & Western United States* map covers the greater Rocky Mountains region. Available from Stanfords – tel. (020) 7836 1321

### USEFUL READING
*Backcountry Bear Basics* by David Smith (Grey Stone Books)

Mount Katahdin is the last leg of
the Appalachian Trail and makes
a fantastic few days' walking.

# BIG IN AMERICA

STATESIDE, THINGS HAPPEN ON A GRANDER SCALE; AND THIS LONG DISTANCE PATH IS NO EXCEPTION. MARTIN VARLEY BIT OFF AS MUCH AS HE WANTED TO CHEW BUT STILL GOT THE FULL WILDERNESS TASTE.

Photography **Martin Varley**

The Appalachian Trail is the mother of long distance footpaths. People were walking it when Wainwright was just a bookkeeper, not a book writer. For decades it was longer than any other route in the world, and it remains a challenge for us Brits, who consider the Pennine Way to be a pretty big undertaking. Walk from Land's End to John O'Groats and back, and you're in the right foot-bruising ball park.

Although the 14 US states the trail crosses are home to eighty million people, it's hardly crowded. It starts in the middle of nowhere – Springer Mountain, Georgia – and finishes equally anonymously on the summit of Mt Katahdin in Baxter State Park, Maine. In the intervening 2,618 miles the closest you get to civilisation is hidden towns such as Erwin, Waynesboro and Troutville. The trail itself traverses a mountain range that's home to one of the world's great hardwood forests and teems with distinctly un-British wildlife: bears, moose, wild boar, snakes and a battalion of less-deadly fauna. The highest peak rises to almost 7,000ft and there are more than 350 peaks over 5,000ft. In just one week you can cross 50 Scafell Pikes.

Any long distance walk is a test of physical and mental endurance, and you can't help wondering what motivates people. Bill Bryson, who wrote of his experiences on the Appalachian Trail in his bestseller *A Walk in the Woods*, says he was driven by a desire to get fit and learn to fend for himself in the wilderness. He tells of amazing feats: like the blind man, Bill Irwin, who hiked the trail with his guide dog and fell down an estimated 5,000 times in the process. Then there's the 'ultra-runner' David Horton who

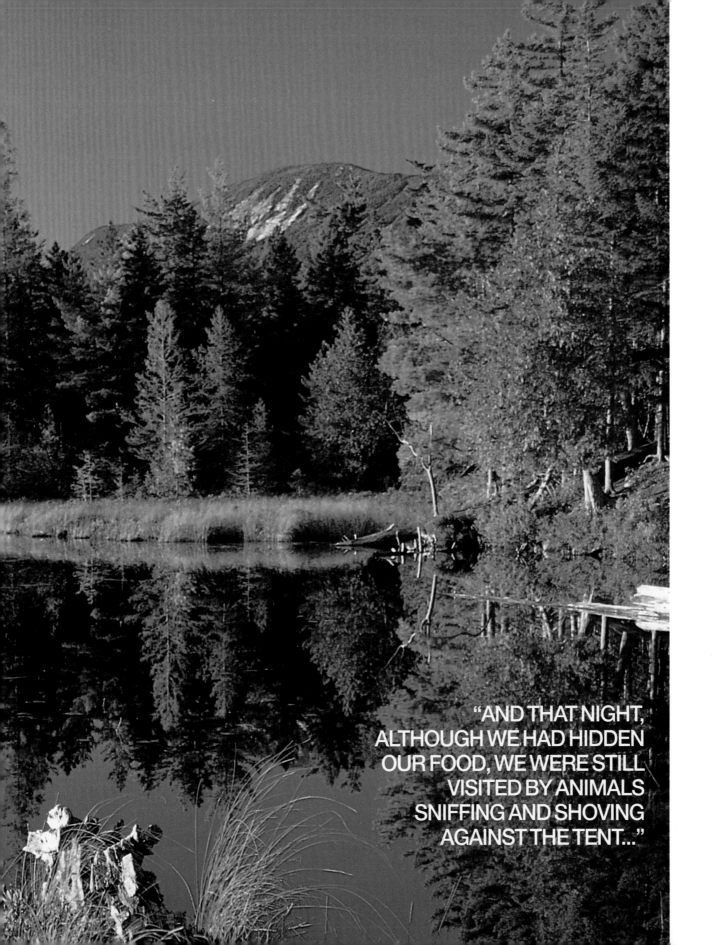

"AND THAT NIGHT,
ALTHOUGH WE HAD HIDDEN
OUR FOOD, WE WERE STILL
VISITED BY ANIMALS
SNIFFING AND SHOVING
AGAINST THE TENT..."

completed it in only 52 days and nine hours. In doing so, he became an emotional wreck and cried for most of the way across Maine.

I didn't want to run the risk of insanity, so there was no question of my attempting the entire route. However, coming from a busy country where the popularity of the fells means that a walk up High Street sometimes seems more like a traipse down Oxford Street, the prospect of a trip into real wilderness was too tempting to pass up. Wife Joanna and I, and our overactive one-year-old daughter Iona, were in Boston to visit a friend who was offering free accommodation and free use of his car. So, after a short stop in the city, we drove north into Maine and headed for Baxter State Park. This, the largest wilderness in the eastern US, is home to huge numbers of moose, among other things.

Indeed, Maine has more moose than any other eastern state; and our hopes of seeing one grew after a stop on the interstate. The source of our information was a stiff, bespectacled pensioner, who sidled over to us asking if we knew what a skunk smelled like. "There's one hell of a stink in my car," he said, pushing his glasses up his nose. "I can only guess it's skunk." Our nasal unfamiliarity with North American mammals let him down, but we got talking; and when he heard we were heading for Baxter State Park, he all but guaranteed we'd see moose.

Late that evening, we arrived at the Appalachian Trail Lodge in Millinocket, the nearest town to the end of the walk. It was full of bearded, wild-eyed men celebrating the completion of their epic adventure. Groups of trekkers who hadn't changed socks for a week sat swapping stories and sizing up each others' blisters. The last section of the route is comfortingly known as the Hundred Mile Wilderness: a week of walking without seeing a shop, a house or a paved road. That would certainly explain the musty stench...

We were short on stories but keen to learn about the section of the trail we were here to walk. The Hundred Mile Wilderness leads to Mt Katahdin, at 5,200ft the highest peak in Maine and the climax of the Appalachian Trail. A handful of routes of varying difficulty thread their way to the summit. From one corner a long, curving, serrated ridge of fractured granite – the Knife Edge – peels away to the east. Barely more than a metre wide in places, this, we were told, was the most spectacular ridge east of the Rockies. However, exposure, dizzying heights and sheer cliffs didn't seem the right combination for someone with a toddler on his back. And anyway, the Appalachian Trail followed the Hunt Trail on the opposite side of the mountain...

A plaque on the door of our room was dedicated to Earl Shaffer, a cult figure in the small world of the Appalachian Trail. In 1948 this man became the first person to walk the entire length of the trail in one summer. Without a tent, and sometimes navigating off only a road map, he completed the route in 123 days, averaging 17 miles a day. Although the trail had been open for years, curiously many people still thought it was not possible to complete the entire journey. Shaffer met virtually no other hikers during his four-month journey, and many local people were not even aware that the trail existed. To cap it all, when he reported his achievement to the trail administrators, they didn't believe him. He had to show them photos and journals (and no doubt till receipts) before his story was finally accepted. Not content with pioneering the trail, Shaffer returned to walk the route 48 years later in 1996, and again in 1998. And here was I, sleeping in the same room, possibly the same bed, as that legend.

By the time we arrived at the park the following day it was already well past moose time. These creatures are reputed to prefer the cool quiet of dawn and dusk. But no sooner had we turned the first corner on our part of the trail than, at the corner of a pond, we saw a moose and her calf. Even the yelps of an excited one-year-

# Up close and personal

LOUISE PARKER

🚶🚶 The Appalachian Trail was completed on 14 August 1934.

🚶🚶 It was the world's first long distance footpath (at the time it was the longest footpath in the world). Today there are two other, longer 'Triple Crown' trails in America: the Pacific Crest Trail and the Continental Divide Trail.

🚶🚶 It passes through 14 states: Georgia, North Carolina, Tennessee, Virginia, West Virginia, Maryland, Pennsylvania, New Jersey, New York, Connecticut, Massachusetts, Vermont, New Hampshire and Maine.

🚶🚶 Every year about 1,500 people set out to walk the trail, mainly from south to north. A third make it to halfway, but only about 200 complete the route. About 60 of these turn round and walk back!

🚶🚶 On the 162 miles of trail through New Hampshire there are 35 peaks over 3,000ft.

🚶🚶 The trail in Maine climbs a total height equivalent to three ascents of Everest.

# Fact file

**How long should it take?** Usually 5-6 months, at about 14 miles a day.

**When should I start?** A northbound hiker needs to start before mid-April to ensure finishing before Baxter State Park closes on October 15. Southwards, don't expect the snows to clear before late May.

**How do I get to the trailheads?** The southern terminus is Springer Mountain, Georgia; the nearest airport is Atlanta, then it's a bus, a taxi and a nine-mile walk to the trailhead (or private companies can take you there from Atlanta). The northern terminus is Mount Katahdin in Baxter State Park. Bangor is the nearest airport, then again it's a bus and a taxi to the trailhead.

**What about accommodation?** Best bet is a tent. Huts and hostels are a rarity. The trail has shelters (raised wooden platforms with a roof) about a day's walk apart, but there is no guarantee that other hikers will not beat you to them.

**I'll need food!** Many hikers arrange for supplies to be sent to pre-determined points along the route. Such maildrops contain about a week's-worth of grub.

**Any more tips?** To find out more, visit the Appalachian Trail Conference website www.atconf.org. Or see the Appalachian Long Distance Hikers Association site (www.aldha.org); you can download a copy of the *Appalachian Trail Thru-Hikers Companion* from here – essential reading if you're thinking of attempting the trail.

Left: Milk time on the side of Mount Katahdin.
Above: "You're my Maine Moose…"

old didn't scare them off. To see this, most people get up well before dawn and pay a local guide £100. We were getting the whole show for free – and the moose and its calf were in no hurry to leave. In fact we didn't even bother with our camera; surely the day would be packed with such moments. As luck would have it, we didn't see another moose for the whole trip.

At Katahdin Stream campground at the foot of Mt Katahdin, affectionately known as 'Big K', we came to realise that wilderness camping obviously means something very different in the States. Picnic tables, rain shelters, flat ground and firewood all take the sting out of a night under the stars, but nothing could diminish the pleasure we felt. Sitting around a campfire under a sky the colour of coal and sprinkled with the dust of stars is surely the essence of the great outdoors. And that night, although we had hidden our food, we were still visited by animals sniffing and shoving against the tent. We sank deeper into our sleeping bags and tried to block the noises out…

The following day we rose early for our ascent of Big K. The route up from the campsite is the last leg of the Appalachian Trail; a pilgrimage to a summit native North Americans believed was guarded by Pamola, a giant storm bird which threatened would-be climbers with unpredictable winds and blinding clouds. As it happens, the park ranger service had its own interpretation of the dangers of climbing Maine's highest mountain. Every hiker is asked to register before climbing and advised to set out by 10.30 in order to be able to return before dark (eight to nine hours is a good time in which to complete the climb). Every day the weather conditions are graded between one and five. If it's above two, climbing beyond the treeline is not recommended. Even before you start the climb there is a nagging feeling that you are back at school. It maybe wilderness, but it isn't freedom.

We set off at 8.30am, on a grade two day, so we could continue without fear of being sent home by a park ranger. The path soon began to climb and the woods closed in. The trek to the treeline was like walking the length of Ennerdale while climbing the height of Snowdon in a corridor of forest. And, as with the rest of the Appalachian Trail, the route was very rough and ready. Often we found ourselves negotiating giant boulders while ducking beneath low branches.

But gradually the trees got smaller and thinned out, and the landscape opened up before us, the vast green canvas of Maine stretching to the horizon. It is hard to comprehend the scale. Maine is the 12th smallest state, but it has more uninhabited forest than any other outside Alaska, most of it visible from the slopes of Mt Katahdin.

A broad ridge led upwards. We had left the trees, but we were not yet out of the woods. The path twisted between huge blocks of sticky granite, perhaps not as hair-raising as the Knife Edge, but still not a place you'd choose to twist an ankle or break a leg.

The last arduous mile crossed a wide plateau. Big K rises out of an almost flat plain and up here, high up on the windswept, treeless summit, there was an incredible sense of elevation. After visiting this area, American writer Henry Thoreau wrote that 'The tops of mountains are the unfinished parts of the globe' – and Katahdin feels as unfinished as any. The path up travels through a range of habitats, but on the summit it is as if a small piece of the Arctic has been transported 1,000 miles south. Bitter winds and freezing temperatures mean that very little can live here, and anything which does grows very slowly.

The wind felt as if its last stop had been Greenland. What had started as a shorts and T-shirt walk in the woods was now a fleece and windproof dash to the summit. A posse of jubilant Appalachian Trailers had already arrived and they were celebrating with champagne miniatures, carried over 2,000 miles from Georgia. Over the last few days we had enjoyed just a mouthful of the refreshment which these hikers had been drinking for the last three months; but as we stood around the summit cairn it didn't make any difference. We all shared the same sweet sense of success of climbing Mount Katahdin and tasting one of the finest long distance paths the world has to offer.

# RIGHT ON TARGET

## TAKE A WEEK OUT TO WALK UNDER AFRICAN SKIES WITH AN ARMED GUIDE FOR COMPANY AND BE BACK AT YOUR DESK ON MONDAY!

Words and photography **Jasper Winn**

I'm never quite sure about guns. Good things? Bad things? I suppose, really, that it all depends on where you are in relation to where the particular firearm whose moral value you're debating at the time is actually pointing. If it's a pistol with its barrel halfway up your left nostril, while some hoodlum relieves you of your wallet, Walkman and trainers, then guns in general will probably seem like a bad idea. But, again, if you're hungry enough and taking the first step towards turning a wild rabbit into stew, then the case for guns might look pretty convincing. It's all a matter of perspective. At first, then, I wasn't sure what I felt about Lameck Luhanga's M-16 automatic rifle. As a game scout in Malawi's Nyika Plateau National Park, much of Lameck's work was patrolling for poachers – and I could appreciate that hefting a gun was part of the job. But while he was acting as my guide I was a little less sure what the point of

Trigger-happy chappy! Jasper's only here for the beer. Oh, and the wildlife, the landscape, the walking, the people, the wild camping...

the rifle was. It seemed highly unlikely that anybody was going to 'poach' me. And the Nyika's fauna, though rich in leopards, hyenas, elephants and other 'big' things, is mainly benign, shy and retiring. A pointy stick or a loud shout would deal with most creatures we were likely to meet.

It was only when we started our march that I worked out that the M-16's primary function, on this trip at least, was as a handy walking-stick. Lameck used its barrel to push aside thorny briars. He employed its length to steady himself when crossing log bridges. He leant on it, hands crossed over its 5.56mm muzzle, when taking a breather. I rather began to wish I was carrying a walking-rifle myself.

Lameck and I were trekking the Livingstonia, a four- to six-day trail that straight-lines from 1800m up on the Nyika Plateau down to the shores of Lake Malawi, roughly 50km away. The Livingstonia is a full African adventure that one can fit into a mere week. The route offers everything: high plateau landscapes, big game viewing, some challenging walking and nights camping wild, as well as stays in a remote village and a missionary station. However, the walk starts with an evening of colonial-style comfort at Chelinda Lodge in the centre of the Nyika Plateau.

Somehow, what with elephants and things, I'd managed to lose two days of my walking time... which I was going to make up on the trail. So at Chelinda I revelled in a last night of excess. I flopped in front of my room's blazing log fire to read through a pile of wildlife guides from the bedside library, scoffed seconds of everything at dinner, downed glasses of wine, and stayed up, talking, far too late.

pine plantation, a couple of dirt roads crossing some 3,000 square kilometres of wilderness, and the lodge and a few other buildings at Chelinda, the Nyika has never been much affected by humans. It's a truly primeval and – because of its altitude – a temperate world. Intimation, perhaps, of what Europe might have been like in the time of the wild ox, the mammoth and the sabre-toothed tiger. Though, up here, it was eland, a herd of elephants, and numerous leopards that made up the 'Neolithic' fauna.

It was animals too, not people, that had laid down many of the tracks which we followed. The passing of thousands of hooves and paws had cut the narrow paths so deep into the land that our boots shuffled along in a groove as if we were jogging along an inverted tightrope. We'd upped our pace a bit, and were at what was normally the first night's campsite, Phata Stream, by lunchtime. Lying in the grass, while we ate sandwiches and cakes, Lameck filled me in on the life of a game scout. He loved and knew about wildlife, but poachers – not the guys with bows and arrows, but the gangs with guns – were the downside of the job. "Two scouts have been killed by poachers, though that was before we got these...," he looked down at the M-16 by his side. "My wife worries very much when I am on patrol because this is a risky job – we can be killed by poachers, snakes, leopards, elephants." He stood up and hefted his pack. We walked on.

After a stiff climb we reached the edge of the escarpment and we could look down as far as the shore of Lake Malawi. As we set off down the thin red line of the trail, Lameck was keen to put into practice something he had learnt from the Phoka tribe. They, apparently, recommend a bent-kneed trot as the least tiring

Early – oh, the horror – the next morning I tucked into a full fry-up breakfast. Departure time was drawing near. With a last cup of coffee still in hand, I shrugged on my small, canvas rucksack. I had a sleeping bag, plate and mug, change of clothes, water bottle, notebook and camera. Lameck was already outside. His rucksack held a light tent, cooking pot, a bag of maize meal and another bag of tiny, dried fish.

We strode off into a landscape that could have been Exmoor or even the South Downs. Bracken brushed our knees. Hills rolled under our feet. Dells dingled. Clouds scudded across the sky, and a stiff wind whistled mournfully across the gun barrel. But where Exmoor might have produced a few rabbits, or a fox or maybe a sprint of deer, here the wildlife was authentic Attenborough. We'd barely topped the first hill before Lameck pointed out a line of eland trailing up a far slope. I spotted a warthog for myself, and we both chorused 'Reedbuck!' as two bounded off through the long grass. Lameck also had an impressive eye for excrement. Within an hour's walking he'd pointed out leopard doo-doo "...you see – full of duiker hair", jackal crap, hyena dung "...white with calcium from bones", and – a real collector's item – aardvark poo.

Apart from a gallery of 3,000-year-old hunter-gatherers' cave paintings, the surreally Scandinavian gloom of a British-planted

method of getting down hills. We jogged on and on, blundering our way through thick woodland, skidding over boulders, tearing our way through thorns, accelerating down deep-cut 'steps' and, always, down, down, down.

Gravity might have been doing most of the work, but I still had 'sewing machine leg,' and searing lungs when we stopped for a breather. The only consolation being that Lameck looked like I felt. "There's the village," he gasped, "Chakaka, of the Phoka tribe." We looked down on a few tiny huts, at the bottom of a valley that seemed only to deepen the further, and faster, we descended. We cantered on down.

It was evening when reached the flat area where the villagers' cash-crop coffee beans were dried on mesh racks. Bottles of 'green' lager in hand, we squeezed around the coffee bean watchman's fire under a tiny lean-to. For supper Lameck was going to knock up a traditional Malawian meal for us. Two local delicacies – fried termites and 'mouse-on-a-stick' – were out of season, so it was going to be *n'sima*. Preparing the maize porridge required huge amounts of stirring and simmering to get the required smooth paste. But then with a sprinkling of dried, pewter-coloured, wood-chip-sized – and textured – fish on top, it was ready to scoop up with our fingers.

Next stop Chakaka village, home to the Phoka tribe.

## "Two local delicacies – fried termites and 'mouse-on-a-stick' – were out of season, so it was going to be *n'sima...*"

A small group of Phoka men had appeared out of the dark. Lying beside the fire, after a second helping of n'sima, I listened to the soft sounds of them talking, in Tumbuka, with Lameck. Sounds that mixed with the splashing of the river. And with the calls of night birds. And, shortly after, with my own snores.

Mext morning, after an icy splash in the stream, and coffee and rice, we set off down the red dirt track. We passed women, in wrap-around chitenjas, whose bright design motifs included stylised elephants, sets of coffee cups and even mobile telephones. With hoes and axes balanced on their bonces, they were heading off to work. Giggling girls balanced buckets of water atop their pates. Two lads, trotting along with us, carried their school's goal posts on their heads. I was beginning to feel that my own noodle, carrying no more than a hat, wasn't pulling its weight. As we walked Lameck taught me Tumbuka. Or at least the simplified version: 'Yewo' – a word which, if repeated enough times, apparently covered "Hello, how'ya doing?…grand day isn't it…anyway, I must be off…so, cheers then." We yewo-ed our way onwards.

Our walk to Livingstonia Mission was becoming a bit of a struggle. The sun rose higher and burnt hotter, our legs ached from the previous day's Phoka trot, and, after we had SAS-ed our way across the high, log bridge that crossed the North Rumphi River, the path rose steeply before us again. In Thunda village we drank beers in the shop next to the shop whose sign read, 'You Are Mostly Welcome'. But still my yewos were losing their verve.

It was mid-morning when we staggered onto the veranda of the Stone House in Livingstonia. Free Church Scots had founded the mission station in 1894, and so Livingstonia was a curious mix of African market and, say, Edwardian Aberdeen. Period houses were dotted among the trees and a large church, with a stained glass window showing Livingstone doing some converting, crowned the hill. There was a technical college, a hospital and a school. In the Stone House I was shown to a darkly ecclesiastical room by Genesis, the earnest manager.

Rather than walk back up onto the Nyika, the exhausted Lameck was going to hitchhike back to the park by road, a trip that could take him days. We had a Fanta together and Lameck set off. I had just discovered from Genesis that all alcohol was banned within 'mission lines.' I watched Lameck hobbling off, and realised that I was going to have to face this new challenge alone. And gun-less.

I wasn't alone for long. I headed down to Manchewe Falls,

Malawi's highest water feature, with two volunteer doctors, Derek and John, and a Northern Irish volunteer teacher, Fiona. We found the falls under the protection of a Mafia of small boys, led by the charismatic Edward. Scrambling over rocks, swinging off creepers and sliding down sandy chutes, we followed him and his *Lord of the Flies* troops around the falls' highlights.

"Hiding cave," announced Edward as we came round a ledge and ducked behind a curtain of falling water into a deep, dark cave. "Big fall," he pointed out as we peered down into a cloud of foam and splashing. "Swimming pool," he trumpeted as we popped out of the bush above a small pool with a Jacuzzi-like whirlpool at one end. A shoal of boys immediately vaulted into the water while Fiona and I waded in to bob around in a roiling maelstrom. Excited lads plummeted past us from the heights, one with such velocity that he tore straight through his ragged shorts so they ended up like a ruff around his neck.

We were eating omelettes and salads at the Lukwe Permaculture Camp, overlooking the falls from a Zen temple-ish al fresco dining room, when I suddenly realised, with horror, that the sun was setting and that I still had 12km to go on foot to reach the lake shore before dark. I yelped an oath, leapt up, threw down a handful of kwacha, pulled on my rucksack and hurtled off. The footpath down cut across the 20 hairpin bends of the Gorode dirt road that looped across the 700m rise of the hill-face. The path took the shortest route as surely as a fall of water, its line pulling me down rock faces, down long sandy gouges, down through twists of trees and shrubs, down the very essence of down-ness, and a bit more down on top of that.

Far behind me the sun was lighting up the Nyika Plateau in a deep red wash, and before me there was the thrudding sound of drums, their pulse accelerating my own heartbeat faster still. Whistles, high whoops and choruses of song rang out from under a stand of shade trees. I shot past the party, catching only a glimpse of bright clothes and lines of dancers and figures beckoning me in, before bursting out of the bush and onto the road at Chitimba

"Ah, *mazungu*, you've just missed one *matola* – that bus is gone," a tailor, busily foot-treadling his sewing-machine, told me, "but there will be another one later." He paused, "Or, certainly, tomorrow." The men gathered around him nodded in agreement. "Certainly, tomorrow, *mazungu*," they echoed. I walked across the road and stuck my thumb out. After an hour a wheezing open lorry carrying sacks of unripe mangos pulled out of the dark. A huddle of figures in the back took my pack and helped me in. There was a chorus of "Yewo! Yewo! Yewo." The lorry accelerated along the sandy lake-shore road towards Mzuzu...

# Three African walks in a week or less

### Morocco Ascent of Djebel Toubkal

It's possible, just, to climb North Africa's highest mountain in a long weekend. Fly to Marrakesh (Royal Air Maroc tel: 020 7439 4361) take a grand taxi to Imlil, stay the night at the Club Alpine Française refuge, start early to overnight or camp at/by the Neltner. Early start for ascent to summit (4167m), and then downhill all the way back to Imlil and hotel or taxi back to Marrakesh. You'd need to be fit and experienced to go this fast and there is a real chance of altitude sickness. Find info for this or longer trips to Toubkal and the Atlas Mountains in *The Rough Guide to Morocco* by Ellingham, McVeigh and Grisbrook. Simply trekking in this area is also fantastic and can be done in a weekend or with Travelbag Adventures who run weekend trips to this area. To contact them – tel. (01420) 541007 or check out www.travelbag-adventures.com.

### Mali Walk the Bandiagra Escarpment in Dogon country

Fly to Bamako/Mopti (Point Afrique ex Paris – tel. (0033) 475 972040 & www.point-afrique.com), jeep to Dogon country and walk 5-6 days on the Bandiagra Escarpment. Nights spent in Dogon villages, where traditional beliefs include funerary mask dances: 12-20km per day with some tough but non-technical ascents. Niger cruise and/or visit to Timbuktu also possible. Saga Tours, a Malian-American tour company based in Mali, can arrange internal transport, village accommodation and guides as well as other itineraries. Visa (from Paris) and yellow fever certificate needed (www.sagatours.com & mail@sagatours.com)

### Uganda Mountain Gorilla Walk

Fly to Entebbe Airport and travel onwards to Queen Elizabeth National Park. Length of walks can be anything from a few kilometres' marching to hours of jungle-bashing, depending on where the gorillas are. The week-long trip also includes game viewing and chimpanzee walk. Price from £1,385 – excluding flights – with Guerba Travel – tel. 01373 858956 & www.guerba.com

MATT SWAINE

# Fact file

## Livingstonia walk in a week

### Itinerary

**Saturday**: fly British Airways (– tel. 0845 773 3377 www.ba.com) ex London to Lilongwe. Evening departure.

**Sunday**: arrive and spend night in Lilongwe.

**Monday:** morning flight to Mzuzu, light plane to Chelinda Lodge, Nyika Plateau.

**Tuesday**: walk to Phata Stream, camp.

**Wednesday**: walk to Chakaka village and camp or lodge.

**Thursday**: walk to Livingstonia, night in Stone House.

**Friday**: walk to Manchewe Falls and night at Lukwe Permaculture Camp.

**Saturday**: walk to Chitimba on Lake Malawi, bus to hotel in Mzuzu.

**Sunday**: morning flight Mzuzu-Lilongwe, sight-seeing, evening flight to UK.

**Monday**: arrive Heathrow circa 5am. Shower, and off to work.

**Season**: April to November

**Time difference:** + 2 hours

**Kit**: You'll need sleeping bag, warm clothing, light rain jacket, good lightweight boots, water bottle. Binoculars for wildlife watching, and take clothes in drab colours if you want to get close. All film, batteries and necessary medical supplies. Insect repellent (100% Deet), high factor sun-cream, hat. You can hire a lightweight tent and cooking pots, or take your own.

**How to arrange:** Contact David or Robyn Foot of Nyika Safaris (reservations@nyika.com) who can arrange the above itinerary, including game scout/guide (compulsory), accommodation, food and domestic air tickets.

Nyika Safaris can also pick up walkers directly from Lilongwe inbound flight with their own plane. If spending more than a week in Malawi, it's possible to add on elephant and wildlife watching in Vwaza Game Reserve, horse riding and game drives on Nyika Plateau, and diving and canoeing from Chinthechi Inn on Lake Malawi.

**Visas**: Not needed for UK, most Commonwealth and most European passport holders.

**Money**: Approx 120 Kwacha to the pound. Change money at airport and take extra cash in US dollars (which are easier to change and can often be used as cash and for tips)

**Language**: Northern Malawians speak Tumbuka; but guides, game scouts and many locals speak English.

**Medical**: Check with a specialist travel medical centre but likely recommendations will be vaccinations against tetanus, polio, typhoid and possibly hepatitis. There is no malaria on the Nyika Plateau due to its altitude but lower down there is chloroquine-resistant malaria. Malarone (prescription-only and expensive) is now recommended by many doctors, and is effective with minimum side effects. As important is to avoid mosquito bites. If spending time on Lake Malawi be aware that there is a risk of exposure to bilharzia in some of its waters.

**Contacts**: Malawi Tourism (UK) for information on all aspects of travel to and within Malawi – tel: (0115) 982 1903 or e-mail enquiries@malawitourism.com.

For information on various walks in Malawi contact Walks Worldwide, (UK), (tel: +44 (0)1524 or www.walksworldwide.com).

**Guidebooks**: Lonely Planet's *Malawi* (Jan 2001) and *Bradt Guide to Malawi*. Both carry warnings against walking from Livingstonia to Malawi Lake, which now seem unnecessary.

# NEARER MY GOD TO THEE

CAN YOU REALLY ATTAIN ENLIGHTENMENT ON A MOUNTAIN?
TREK TO THE WORLD'S HOLIEST HILL AND YOU'LL FIND OUT...

Words & photography **Ben Winston**

Fluttering prayer
flags frame
Kailash's north face.

Last time you climbed Helvellyn, did you find God? What about Ben Nevis – did you find Him there, shivering in the emergency shelter and trying to locate itinerant satellites on His GPS? No, I suspected as much. But if you had a large stone tablet for every time you found mountains mentioned in the mythologies of the world's great religions, you'd be able to build another Everest or a very big church at least. This is because mountains and religion have been linked since long before Moses trouped up Mount Sinai for a cloudy convention with Yaweh. From the very dawn of time they have held up the sky, offered a mutual platform for God and man to meet, passed landslide judgment and granted river redemption, offered peaceful retreat to countless sages and holy men, and confronted walkers and climbers with humbling forces and long views to instil a heightened perspective on life. They have earned their rightful place in religion.

Apart from religions based within the strict geographical confines of Holland, almost every creed holds one peak or another holy. In China, for example, Buddhists worship four mountains that are home to bodhisattvas, spiritual creatures who dedicate themselves to helping all sentient beings reach enlightenment. And there are at least seven mountains venerated by the ancient mystical belief system of Taoism. Mount Fuji, the enigmatic Japanese volcano, draws thousands of white-robed, straw-hatted Shinto pilgrims every year. Then there's Olympus, home of the Greek gods; or the four sacred mountains of the Navajo. There's Nepal's fish-tailed Machapuchare, Ireland's Croagh Patrick, or India's Nanda Devi… the list just goes on. But there is one little-known summit that stands head and shoulders above the rest. It lies pretty much unnoticed by the western world in distant Tibet, yet it's the holiest mountain on earth.

Mount Kailash is revered by over a billion Hindus. It is the centre of the universe for Tibetan Buddhists, Jains and Bonpo, and has been the great spiritual enigma for countless adventurers who for centuries have worked hard to cross an inhospitable landscape to catch sight of it. In terms of the sheer weight of worshippers this makes it the very holiest of holies, although for pragmatic walkers such as myself it offers an adventure unparalleled by anything else in this life, and quite possibly the next. Best of all, you can reach enlightenment by walking around it; and in spite of seas that cure cancer and valleys where life is eternal, there aren't many geological phenomena that offer you that.

I set off for Kailash hoping to achieve this enlightenment. That is, not only to reach God and the kingdom of heaven but, according to the Buddhist version, to actually become God as well. It seemed like an exciting prospect: unlimited power in heaven and earth, omniscience, omnipresence and eternal freedom from blisters. But achieving it was never going to be easy because, according to

Tibetan Buddhism, while one circuit (or kora) of the mountain absolves the sins of a lifetime, it takes 108 circuits to earn your enlightenment – no mean feat when each kora is 30 miles and at an average altitude of Mont Blanc. But fate was on my side because during the auspicious Tibetan Year of the Horse, each kora is worth the spiritual equivalent of 13 circuits completed in non-horse years. Which meant that during 2002, I had only to complete 8.3 circuits for the ultimate reward.

But before Nirvana there was the material world to deal with and at Darchen, the shabby village of mud houses and pilgrim tents where the kora starts and finishes, it felt like much of the material world was coming out of my arse. This is because Tibet is an unhealthy country. The latrines are renowned throughout Asia for their despicable state – crap on the floor, walls and sometimes even the ceiling – and to visit them (particularly at night) induces a state of paranoia familiar to those who clear mine fields for a living. Illness is commonplace and death is much closer than in the hygienic west. And when at the beginning of my first week I set off on my first *kora*, I was ill and feeling closer to death than is normal for a Monday morning. As a result I decided to go lightweight, exchanging my tent for a sheet of clear plastic and leaving my down jacket behind; but it would take much more than a diminished rucksack to get me around the mountain.

This is because the trouble with Tibet is the altitude. At an average of 4000m, it's a land that owes its unique character to the time when India slammed into mainland Asia, threw up the Himalayas by way of a crumple zone, and pushed the Tibetan plateau onto the roof of the world. It means that the world's largest peaks shield Tibet from the monsoon that keeps Nepal so green, leaving the plateau (which is almost the size of western Europe but with fewer than 3 million inhabitants) an inhospitable and dry high-altitude desert, full of mountains. Darchen lies at around 4600m and walking there for the uninitiated is like going for an uphill run and breathing only through your nose. Or sucking the thick milkshake of life through a very thin straw – exhausting and frustrating. I was lucky though, for an extended period of acclimatisation had spared me the worst effects of altitude and left me marginally freer to appreciate the awesome scenery. And awesome it was. This is because Darchen sits on the edge of a plain so vast and flat that it looks like a holy vision with a frozen meringue of Himalayan peaks on its far edge. It also sits right beneath the dusty hills of the Kailash range which loom up in a bout of most improbable geology: purples and blues and yellows that really have no rightful place in the normal colour scheme of rocks. It is a landscape calculated to make even the most devout atheist believe in That Which Lies Beyond; but for me it was the first sight of Kailash that left me knowing what it is like to believe – to truly believe – in something not dissimilar to God.

The south face of Kailash is made out of sapphire, the west face ruby, the north face gold and the east face crystal. Although from where I stood an hour out from Darchen I couldn't see the precious stone for the sloping face of snow (beneath which the rock looked suspiciously like conglomerate), there was no doubting the beauty of this mountain. A lone snow-capped peak with four distinct faces, each corresponding – uncannily – to one of the cardinal directions, it was easy to see how it commands such widespread worship. The Tibetans see it as a huge mandala, or deity used during meditation to focus the mind, although it is also the site of Tibetan Buddhism's defeat of the older religion of Bön Po in a great magical contest between saints. For Hindus it is the home of destroyer and fertility god Lord Shiva, plus his beautiful consort Parvati. It is also meant to represent a *Shiva-lingam*, or Shiva's penis; but, to be honest, and in spite of the monolithic nature of the mountain, you'd have to have a pretty sketchy idea of the phallus to see it. For both religions,

Tibet has an average altitude of 4000m so the going is far from easy.

Darchen: "A shabby village of mud houses and pilgrims tents."

Dharma bum: sleeping under a plastic sheet and camera tripod tent.

The north face of Kailash: the holiest mountain in the world?

A Buddhist mani stone, found all over the Himalayas.

In the Year of the Horse a little over eight koras buys enlightenment.

Girl in Darchen: the start and finish of each kora.

And you're impressed by the London Marathon runner in the rhino suit...

though, Kailash is the centre of the universe, the *axis mundi*, or world pillar that links the physical plane and the spiritual with the depths of hell below. That's how important it is. Yet for me, Kailash represented something entirely different. In spite of the respect I held for these other beliefs, the mountain was simply a mountain: a gorgeous mountain, a mountain in one of the most remote and beautiful places on earth. That it had taken so much time and effort to reach was part of what made it sacred, as was the fact that climbers have, in spite of Chinese permission, refused to climb the mountain in deference to its hallowed status. I liked that. I liked the fact that there are still some things that command more respect than our quasi religious notion of personal achievement. I like that those things are other people's beliefs, and mountains.

But personal achievement was what my trip was all about and ten miles into the kora, I experienced deep personal failure and collapsed. Illness, altitude and too heavy a rucksack had taken their toll. It was then that an angel appeared, a lone Tibetan, a huge shaggy bear of a man with a red braid woven into his plait and wrapped around his head. He sat down next to me and I offered him my food, then when I came to leave he wrestled me for my rucksack. There was nothing I could do. I watched as he shouldered my load, threw his own small bundle of rags over his shoulder and then motioned me to follow. It was an act of remarkable kindness, but kindness is a plague in Tibet which proves that in spite of the oppression and genocide inflicted by the

Three years, 1,000 miles of crawling and bowing, and not one paracetamol...

Chinese – vicious enough to brew hatred in the most pious of saints – Tibetans have an unbelievable capacity for humanity and love. And there must be some sort of lesson in that.

Next morning I woke to find a golden marmot staring at me. It was probably wondering why I was there in the open, a little nose poking through a hole in a sleeping bag covered with a thick crust of hoar frost. The thermometer read -11 deg C. I was camped not far from the path where hundreds of Tibetans were filing past, wrapped tight in yak wool robes and each wearing a funky hat, and they stared at me with even more curiosity than the marmot. Mad, they must have been thinking, but I knew I wasn't anything like as mad as some of them because later that day I discovered one of the strangest human activities on the planet. In an act of utter devotion, some pilgrims were prostrating themselves around the mountain in a three-week blitz of praying, kneeling and spreading themselves out on the floor, rubbing their foreheads in the dirt, standing up and doing it all again. And if that wasn't strange enough, there was one man who had prostrated himself from the capital city of Lhasa, over 1,000 miles away. Three years of crawling and bowing had left him with a large fleshy protrusion on his forehead, but it just goes to show what people will do for mountains and for God.

Shiva and Parvati opt for an 'early night'.

## Fact file

### Kailash

The mountain is in the far west of Tibet and the easiest way of visiting is with an organised tour. Himalayan Kingdoms is currently running the tour for around £3,500 – www.himalayankingdoms.com or tel. (01453) 844400. A much cheaper alternative is to make your way to Kathmandu (where almost all treks to Tibet begin) and contact the excellent and reliable Karnali Excursions who are specialists in Kailash and western Tibet – www.trekkinginnepal.com, or email karnali@excrns.wlink.com.np

Qatar Airways runs daily flights to Kathmandu. Ask about free membership to the Adventure Club which entitles you to a useful extra 10kg baggage allowance. Tel. 0870 770 4215 or visit www.qatarairways.com

*Tibet*, pb Lonely Planet is the most useful up-to-date reading on the country and has a good section on the Kailash kora. Also check out Gary McCue's *Trekking in Tibet*, pb The Mountaineers – a superb book with lots of trek and background detail, but hideously out of date for practical travel.

## Some other holy mountains for you to try...

### Sinai

Where God gave Moses the Ten Commandments, but also important in Islam as the place where Mohammed's horse Boraq ascended to heaven. Although there is debate as to which of 20 possible peaks is the actual biblical summit, Egyptian Mount Musa is generally accepted as the place. At 2637m it's an accessible mountain with 3,750 steps to the top, carved by the monks of St Catherine's Monastery, the possible location of Moses's burning bush.

### Fuji

At 3776m and with a world-famous symmetry, Fuji is Japan's tallest and most popular mountain. It is actually made up of three different volcanoes superimposed upon one another; and, if you look carefully, you can see evidence of them. Shinto pilgrims often ascend the mountain wearing white clothes and broad straw hats, ringing a bell and chanting: "May our six senses be pure, and the weather on the honourable mountain fair." Which it often is.

### Olympus

Home to the Greek Gods and the highest mountain in the country at 2917m. Well known for its skiing in the winter, the summit of Olympus was first reached in 1913 by Christos Kakalos from nearby Litohoro and a couple of Swiss mountaineers: Frederic Boissonas and Daniel Baud-Bovy. These days thousands of people climb it every year in one or two days. Accessible from both Athens and Thessaloniki.

Two days later and after a 5630m pass, I emerged from the valleys and canyons that circle the mountain to discover a mini enlightenment that was mostly due to relief. The trek had indeed been a religious experience: unholy hard work, a rising from the (almost) dead, plenty of prayers to whatever god would listen and a sickness-induced fast in the wilderness. I had seen angels, experienced hell and on more than one occasion held aloft a single finger to the holy hill, wondering whether the lack of lightning proved either the compassion or the non-existence of God. But stepping out back onto the plain with the 7728m Gurla Mundata dominating the far skyline and with the sun turning a miraculous colour to the west, there was, finally, an understanding between me and the world that went some way to being religious.

I kept going around the mountain for another month, sometimes getting up before dawn with a thousand murmuring pilgrims and completing the kora in a day; other times strolling easy and sleeping in nomads' tents or poky monasteries, eating with Tibetans the dried goat's flesh from carcasses curing on the walls. To be surrounded by so much devotion and piety was a humbling experience that put scepticism into sharp relief; I was awed by the religious fervour that made these people walk endless loops of a mountain in the hope of a better reincarnation. And if I couldn't believe in their Buddhism, nor Shiva and Parvati getting up to God knows what on top, I couldn't deny the power of that mountain. It was right at the core of what we were all doing out there in the middle of nowhere; a bloody great big hill, a monolith, a deity, an enormous lump of inert rock which we all circled and onto which we projected our needs for belief.

As for the enlightenment, well, that's another, much longer story. Suffice to say I now know there are some mountains that do have incredible power over humans, and some religions that have even more power than that. But in our modern era of globalisation and technological warfare we could do worse than listen to the words of a long distance Hindu walker who told me: 'Respect all, but worship your own.' Not the wisest words ever uttered, it's true, but the route to Nirvana is a long one. And as someone much wiser once said: 'the longest journey begins with a single step.'

# PADDLE AND SADDLE PATAGONIA

WHERE ELSE CAN YOU PLAY AT BEING A COWBOY ONE DAY AND KAYAK
BETWEEN ICEBERGS THE NEXT?  ADVENTURE WALKING IN CHILE…

Words & photos **Jasper Winn**

Patagonia's a bit of a long way to go for a walk. In fact I'd guess that most British trekkers think of Patagonia, when it troubles their minds at all, as a handy metaphor for off-this-planet, never-coming-back remoteness. Which is understandable because, though it may have all the history, myth and geographical furniture of a stand-alone country, 'Patagonia' is no more than an imprecise label for those chunks of Chile and Argentina lying south of the 42° line of latitude. Patagonia seems, and perhaps is, more of a concept – a sort of Timbuktu with rain – rather than an actual place one might think of flying to for a few weeks of pleasant strolling.

Yet a surprisingly large number of British travellers, intent on plying their Vibram soles, do head to Chilean Patagonia. Or, more specifically, they overfly the dull stuff – the immense, flat grasslands which have all the allure of Belgium-sized pieces of sisal matting, and the million hectares of the Southern Ice Field that form the biggest slab of badly defrosted natural fridge outside the Poles – and touch down far to the south for a bracing yomp around the Torres del Paine National Park. And it's a smart move.

Because, quite simply, if Patagonia is everything below South America's knees, then the Torres hangs around the subcontinent's very shapely ankle, in a chain of jewel-like peaks, glittering glaciers and sapphire lakes. The park arguably packs more gobsmacking, brutally impressive scenery into its 2,400 square kilometres than any other comparable area in the world. It's as if God had scrunched the best bits of Alaska, Norway and Iceland into an area small enough to walk the highlights of in a fortnight; but with

enough wonders to keep one busy, even as a full time gob-smackee, for a month. Or a year. Or a decade.

The Torres landscape is spectacular. Twenty and more peaks soar above the 2000m mark, cathedralling up from dead flat plains or springing out of their own reflections in the silvered lakes. Glaciers squeezing out like fresh-mint toothpaste between the molars and incisors of the massifs' jaws. Torrenting rivers freighting icebergs down to the sea. There are deeply gouged valleys, tangled forests of southern beech, wide grasslands. And always the mountains. The names tell you plenty about their shapes and sizes. Los Torres, Los Cuernos and Los Cumbres. The 'towers,' the 'horns' and, the 'summits,' which ironically – do the Chileans do ironic? – includes the highest peak of them all, the 3050m Cumbre Principal.

And then there's the wildlife. Regular condor fly-bys. Herds of ballerina-limbed guanaco. Two flavours of fox. Gooseberry-green Austral parakeets. Shrimp-pink Chilean flamingoes wading the edge of jade-enamelled lakes, before turning into rippling scarlet slashes as they take flight. Ñandu – ostrich-like and barely smaller – stalking around the pampas with the aggressively bored concentration of traffic wardens. And you probably have as much chance of seeing a puma, here in the Torres, as anywhere in the world.

Make the long journey down to the Torres once and you risk becoming Patagonian-ised. It's happened to me: two trips so far, and both times only the winter snows drove me out. Some people I met return year after year. Others had just given in, started businesses and stayed down there through every summer.

## "It's as if God had scrunched the best bits of Alaska, Norway and Iceland into an area small enough to walk... in a fortnight..."

Patagonia's extremes of weather are infamous.

Refugios – like this one at Zapata – mean you don't need to pack a tent.

Alec Quevedo and Lian Hayes, the American/Ecuadorian and English founders of Blue Green Adventures, first came to the Torres a decade ago. Since then they've been leading trips in and around the park, using horses and kayaks, as well as walking, to take the intrepid to those areas most other people never reach.

Alec was evangelical about travellers – not just his clients – getting the most out of the park. "It's crazy to come all this way and then just walk on the two or three most popular trails with everybody else," he told me. "Yeah, of course they're good treks – that's why they're so popular – but there's so much else to do. It makes sense to go further, to get out to the working estancias on a horse, paddle one of the rivers, and do the walking as well."

A horse is the key to getting off the well-trodden trails in the Torres. Luckily, Patagonia has good horses. The four-leg-drive local Criollo can gallop for kilometre after kilometre, scramble up rock faces and swim rivers, dodging the icebergs as it goes. They don't need fancy riding skills, and their saddles are draped in sheepskins for Pullman seat comfort. Horses are what the locals use for getting around on, as well as for herding sheep and packing supplies to the park's *refugios*, ranger stations and scientific camps.

The Patagonian cowboys – *baqueanos* – are horse-opera heroes, trousered in voluminous *bombachos*, booted and spurred, hung about with shawls and knives and lassos. They're good guys to ride with: tough, fun and knowledgeable about their land and its wildlife. Their favoured headgear is the Benny Hill beret – about the only hat that can resist Patagonia's scouring gales and storms.

The south of Patagonia can produce more 'weather' in a day than most other landscapes manage to scrape together in a year. Sun, snow, rain and wind. The lot. Especially wind. "I came over the pass and my contact lens blew right out of my eye," one English walker complained to me, when I met him on a, by local standards, moderately blustery day. "But," he added, "I found it stuck to a rock, 20 foot away – luckily it was glittering in the sun." I must have met 10 people who'd been knocked off their feet by blasts of wind. One woman even claimed her horse had been blown over. Weather stories in Patagonia are like drinking stories in Ireland – the currency of travellers' conversation. Most don't need exaggeration.

For the first three days of a nine-day ride around the National Park, cold rain fell solidly. If I'd breathed too heavily, I'd have drowned. Still, a bunch of us were sitting on top of sopping wet horses to get to the glacier at Pingo Lake. The night before we'd ridden up through the southern beech forests, camped out at the clapboard hut at Zapata, and cooked up a pot of stew. Shirts and socks dried around the stove. The world and our lives were washed in the sepia tones of a 19th century Daguerreotype of early cowboy pioneers. Finally reaching the lake, we broke off chunks of 2,000-year-old ice to put in our shots of whiskey. "One time we came up here in a warm spell and the only 'bergs for the drinks' ice

## People

**Nelly Gelich, New South Wales, Australia**
"I've got a panoramic feature on my camera – you know, a wide-angle – and I still have to take six shots to get all this view in."

**Alexandra Muñoz, Santiago, Chile**
"The best thing about the park? Oh, the environment, the mountains,

the glaciers – every corner of it is magical for me. It's not that difficult to come here – even for Europeans – and it's not cold either… people think it's like the South Pole, and it's not; we're in March now and look how good the weather is."

**Oliver Hume, London**
(after a particularly long day in the saddle, over rough ground)
"Ah, death – it's looking like an enticing option. Isn't it lucky I have a drop of whiskey handy for emergencies."

**Reneé Hall, Utah, USA**
"The *refugios* are a very nice find – not having to drag along a tent, and to be able to get a hot shower and a warm bed, and not worry about pumas. I didn't want to completely separate from civilisation or have to go six days without a shower."

**Paola, Alejandra, Lito, Christian, Marcos and Julio**

**– Chilean staff in Los Cuernos *refugio* (talking together)**
"The oldest person we've had staying was 84 years old, *un ingles* – he had his birthday here – he was walking the 'W' trail, without a problem. And the youngest person was four months old. No! No! *Hombre*, there have been younger: think of the pregnant women who have stayed here."

**Mireille van Kessel, Netherlands**
"We had to walk out after the big rain storms, from up near the Towers. We had to cross flooded rivers, and there was always 'BANG! BANG!' from big rock falls. And when we got down to the Torres campsite, then we heard that the Chileano bridge had fallen

down just, maybe, fifteen minutes, half an hour after we crossed it. We didn't expect so much adventure in Patagonia, we were thinking more a little bit of sun, some glaciers, but, no, not so much adventure."

**Paul O'Reilly, UK**
"I think a lot of the people who came without really good waterproofs or warm kit found it tougher, but I actually expected it to be maybe a bit wilder or colder, so I was well prepared even when the weather got a bit tough."

**Philip Lund-Conlon, London**
"We've learnt a few lessons about the right equipment one needs – particularly waterproofs. The weather was incredibly changeable, so we experienced trekking in sun, snow, high winds and rain – the whole gamut – and we were a little bit under-prepared."

**Pamela Horne, Scotland**
(honeymooning with husband Chris)

"I've done a lot of walking in Scotland, in the Highlands, and the park is comparable, it's that level of difficulty. So if you can walk a Scottish Munro you could easily do the 'towers walk' here – same landscape, same weather, same heights. There were a lot of people on the route we took – more than you'd come across on a Scottish Munro."

**Angela Chapman, London**
"It was great at the end of the day to see the *refugio* below. We were always very happy to get across the hill, then sit around the fire, drink wine, swap stories. It was definitely a good combination, to have the wilderness and the *refugios*. Not having done this kind of thing before I wouldn't have liked to camp. I liked being safe in the knowledge that I was going to be warm, could get dry, get a meal after a long day's walk."

**Amanda Camp, Woking** "The weather? Well, all the books we had read had said that the end of March is probably one of the best times to go, and you get good weather, but they didn't say, I certainly wasn't under the impression, that it would be snowing. But I absolutely love it down here, it's so clean and fresh, just lovely."

**Anonymous girl after a week of galloping**
"This place is just amazing especially on horse back. I've already worn out one bra on this trip so far."

Baqueanos with mutton, on the trail and playing at being Annie Oakley.

were way off shore," Alec told us, "One of the baqueanos unhitched his lazo and roped an iceberg in to land just like he'd catch a cow." As he talked the rain was watering down our whiskies nicely.

By the afternoon, though, the sun had come out, waterproofs were tied behind our saddles, and we set off on a long, rolling gallop across the lowland pampas. The peaks of the Paine Grande made up the northern horizon, its jagged serrations ripping into a tight-guyed flysheet of luminous blue sky. Don, a Vietnam veteran who'd barely ridden before the trip, was out on the flank, a smile splitting his face, his camera tripod hitched across his back like a bazooka. Hares and snipe exploded from under our horses' hooves like fur 'n' feather landmines. The hot, sweet smell of sun drying the last drops of rain from the grass filled the air. Don, Holly, Janet, Marcia and the rest of us were intoxicatedly happy as our horses rocked and thudded under us. When we finally pulled to a halt, Holly was the first to speak – or more gasp; "Ooooh! Man!" She was definitely gasping; "Oh, I have just cantered my brains out." Walking a rucksack over a similar distance might have been fun. Even a lot of fun. But, really, not half as much fun as that.

But most people do come to the park to walk. And they do tend to trek one of the two most popular trails, the roughly eight-day 'big circuit,' or the five days or so up and down the 'W.' Both are rewarding and challenging routes to follow as they wind tightly around the mountains' flanks. From them you'll smell the granite and see the wind whipping the snow off the summits in swirling contrails. You'll hear the rolling 'THRUMMPPS' of avalanches falling from the cornices high above the valleys. And you'll definitely see condors turning slow cartwheels through the sky.

Take those trails, though, and you'll also, in all but the low season, meet plenty of other people seeing and hearing the same things. Some 60,000 visitors a year get down this far, and though plenty just take a tour bus on one of the few dirt roads into the park to look at Grey Lake and its icebergs, plenty more are out there camping or staying in the refugios and footing it across the landscape. I headed off to join them on a stroll up and down a couple of the W's legs in early April.

Winter was getting close. I'd waxed my boots, and bought some dried fruit and a bottle of pisco – 40° proof spirit – in Puerto Natales. I had a bivvy bag and inadequate waterproofs, and technically, according to park rules, shouldn't have been walking alone. But, seemingly, I was still better prepared than many. In my first hours of walking from the Torres campsite towards the Cuernos refugio, I ran into a quartet who I'd last seen in Natales' only karaoke bar. They'd already had an adventure. On their first night in the park they'd got lost in the dark on a tree-covered hillside. Kerry, the English quarter of the foursome, described their self-rescue technique: "We couldn't see a thing, so we wrapped Stefan's shirt round a stick and set fire to it, and then his T-shirt,

then another shirt." All available clothing burnt, they next fired off the red-eye reduction flashes on their cameras, running forwards into the brief nanoseconds of strobing light.

Finally, batteries dead, they navigated by the stars. "We found Castor and Pollux, the heavenly twins…" Kerry explained. Stefan added, "…yes, and they pointed right at the camp." I missed the smart science in their take on astronomy. But, still, they were alive and seemed to have displayed a fair amount of initiative in the face of bad luck. Or so I thought, until one of them spotted my map. "Oh, can we have a look at that?" There was a sheepish grin: "Uh, 'cos we haven't actually got one and we don't know where we are."

In the Cuernos refugio that evening there were hunks of boiled mutton for dinner. A five-stringed guitar. Mugs of wine. Forty campers and hostellers. And 40 more stories. Stories of lost trails. Blisters. Sprained ankles. River crossings. Temperature drops. Rain. Hunger. Most were the stories of those who, on a whim, had hired kit in Natales, jumped on a bus and found themselves on an unplanned walk, and dependent on their own feet and common sense for the first time – the paradox of the 'signposted wilderness'.

Early one morning, just few days after finishing the walk, I pulled on a nylon blouse, a rubber skirt and some frankly fetishistic mittens. I gave a little twirl. "How do I look in this?" I asked Pamela and Chris, a Scottish couple who were in Patagonia for a fortnight of riding, walking and kayaking. They too were pulling themselves into the masochistic-bondage outfits of the next-stop-Antarctica ice paddler. Only the day before, we, Alec and Fransisco the river guide had ridden a conveyor belt of zinc grey river current for 50km down the Rio Serrano.

Now, after a camp breakfast, we were ready to launch the two double sea kayaks onto the waters below the snout of the Serrano Glacier. Blocks of ice bobbed around the kayaks as we paddled towards the ice wall. A thick fog hung between the dark cliffs above us, hiding the bulk of the glacier from view. But there was the occasional muffled and soft sounding CRUUUUMMMMP of an avalanche from high up in the cold heavens, as we threaded ourselves between the towering white and blue blocks of ice. Strands of mist curled off the water's surface. Dipping my blade in and pushing us onwards, I felt like the ferryman chap who rows the dead across the river Styx. Except the afterlife was proving to be much colder than I'd imagined it might be. Oh, and much, much more beautiful and haunting.

Patagonia is a long way to go for a walk, but add some 'paddle and saddle' time and it suddenly seems a lot closer. Where else can you walk one of the planet's great long distance trails, play at being a cowboy, and kayak among icebergs? Do all three in the one trip and you've got a bargain. And the weather – that's the family-sized, party-mix pack of weather – you get for free.

# Fact file

**THE BASICS** No visa needed for UK passport holders; a 90-day tourist card is issued when you enter the country (though Australian, Canadian and American passport holders pay a fee). No vaccinations necessary.

**MONEY** Take a supply of US dollars in various denominations and a debit/credit card such as Visa. There are ATMs outside most banks in Chile, even in smallish towns.

**LANGUAGE** It's worth learning at least some Spanish. If you're going off the obvious routes you need to be able to get info on weather, trails and problems ahead. On the well-trodden trails most people who work in tourism have some English, and some have a lot, but start meeting up with cowboys, shepherds and many of the park wardens and it's Spanish or nothing.

**UK AGENTS** To book Blue Green Adventures' 'Best of Three – kayaking, walking and riding' and long distance riding trips in and around the Torres del Paine National Park, contact Last Frontiers, UK – tel. (01296) 653000; e-mail: info@lastfrontiers.com; website: www.lastfrontiers.com. Can arrange international and internal flights.
**GETTING THERE** LanChile, British Airways, Iberia (spectacularly unreliable) and a number of other airlines fly to Santiago ex-UK via various routes (so you can add a stay in Brazil or Argentina to your trip depending on carrier). With LanChile flights it's easier to add the necessary internal flights

to/from Punta Arenas. Try Trailfinders – tel. (020) 7938 3939; www.trailfinders.co.uk for best deals. From Punta Arenas there are buses to Puerto Natales (3-4 hour), the jumping-off point for the park.

It's also possible to do one leg of the trip down the Patagonian coast, to/from Puerto Montt to Puerto Natales, by ship – the three-day voyage can be rough but has stunning views if it's not foggy.

**WHEN TO GO** It's the southern hemisphere so just flip the northern seasons through 180°, exaggerate our winds, sun, rain and cold, to get an idea of what each month will be like. Late April to October is very seriously nippy, and everything in the park and most outfits in Puerto Natales close down, so not a good time to go. Christmas and through January is best avoided as the busiest season with commensurately high air fares, If you're properly equipped ('cos winter'll be a-coming) then March into early April can provide the greatest variety of climate and few people, yet with *refugios* still functioning.

**EQUIPMENT** For camping you'll need good kit – mountain quality tent would be good, plus at least three-season bag and full-length insulation mat and some form of stove. For *refugio* stays you'll still need a sleeping bag, and an emergency bivvy bag would be a very wise precaution. In theory you can hire all the kit you need for whichever sleep option you choose in Puerto Natales, as well as waterproofs and boots, but it's difficult to find good or even adequate quality kit. Whichever month you visit

the park, you'll need full waterproofs, good boots and gaiters plus a few warm layers, and at least one back-up dry set, as well as gloves and a warm hat that'll stay on in high winds. Double-wrap everything in your pack in plastic bags. Paradoxically, you'll also need sunglasses, insect repellent and sun cream for hot days. You can do a day or two of riding in a pair of jeans and lightweight walking boots for riding, but for longer trips comfy trousers and practical riding footwear are recommended.

**GUIDEBOOKS** *Rough Guide Chile*, and Lonely Planet's *Chile and Easter Island*. *The Bradt Guide to Trekking in Chile and Argentina* by Tim Burford. Lonely Planet's *Trekking in the Patagonian Andes* (Feb 1998, £11.99) is worth considering.

## PUERTO NATALES

**ACCOMMODATION** Natales has everything from four-star hotels to dormitory accommodation. Hostal Concepto Indigo – tel. +56 (0)61 413609 & www.conceptoindigo.com is a good mid-range, one-stop option: restaurant, bar, Internet connections and reliable information on the park. Or for a cheaper room, and relaxed family atmosphere, try Residencial Anita, Chorrillos 830 – tel. +56 (0)61 415802 & e-mail: anita@nataleslodge.cl

**SERVICES** There are a number of banks with ATM machines, two good chemists, numerous Internet cafes, and shops selling everything from slide film

to saddles. Dried fruits, cheeses and other trail foods are available in supermarkets. Good restaurants, plenty of bars and regular rodeos make the town a good place for end-of-trip rewards.

**TOUR OPERATORS** For riding in the park contact Baqueano Zamora, Calle Eberhard 566 (– tel. +56 (0)61 413953 & baqueanoz@terra.cl) who are also local agents for Blue Green Adventure's week and longer rides (camping or staying on ranches), and their 'Best of Three' trips. Zamora can also arrange local transport, tours, guides and accommodation in the park.

For kayak trips (one to several days) contact Fransísco López (– tel. +56 (0)61 415885 & rutaspatagonia @entelchile.net).

Ice-climbing is done on Grey Glacier through the Hostal Concepto Indigo.

**PARK DETAILS** Numerous daily scheduled buses to the park entrance (115km away). The more expensive taxis and tour buses can take you via the Milodón cave en route, if you're a fan of Chatwin's *In Patagonia*. The main park entrance is at Laguna Amarga where you need your passport to check in. You pay a fee and declare what kit you have; when you leave the park, even if by another route, you must ensure you sign out to save a search (admittedly very unlikely) for the 'missing' you, at your cost.

From the entry you can take the minibus to the Hosteria Las Torres hotel, *refugio* and campsite, or to the catamaran that heads for the Pehoe *refugio* and camping, depending on which direction you're walking the routes. Bring all the food you'll need.

**ACCOMMODATION** Hosteria Mirador del Payne, Estancia Lazo (– tel. +56 (0)61 228712, e-mail: payne@ mundosur.com & www.mundosur. com/payne).

**MAPS** There are adequate maps for sale in Puerto Natales; best (and laminated) is probably the *Mapa de Excursionismo Parque Nacional Torres del Paine* (Chileguide, February 1999) which shows all the important features and details at 1:100,000 (1cm to 1km), though there have been some trail re-routings since its publication.

**MEDICAL** Few problems, bar hypothermia and the kind of physical dangers that come with a rugged landscape and remote areas. A sprained ankle, or worse, can herald a bit of a drama to get you out, and considerable expense (check your insurance); note that the rescue helicopter based in Punta Arenas is very often grounded due to bad weather, so you'd be hauled out by guys and horses. People do die in the park – usually by falling off things – rather than puma attack. There's plenty of water about, but use common sense in which you choose to drink.

**MOBILE PHONES** (thank God) don't work here. So look after yourself, talk to your real neighbours and stop hollering into a bit of over-priced plastic and microchippery.

# STAND FIRST

KOREA IS A COUNTRY WITH A DISTINCT PERSONALITY SPLIT DOWN THE 38TH PARALLEL, BUT YOU CAN BE SURE OF TWO THINGS. YOU'LL DEFINITELY MEET MR. KIM, AND THE WALKING IS NOTHING SHORT OF SUPERB!

Photography **Nigel Jenkins**

Rock pinnacles in the Sorak-san National Park.

Trekking through woods on the ascent to Taech'ongbong.

Giant bronze Buddha in Shinhungsa Temple, Sorak-san.

The infamous 38th Parallel.

**"THE 38TH PARALLEL WAS A US-PROPOSED LINE OF DIVISION BETWEEN NORTH AND SOUTH KOREA AFTER WW2. IT WAS THE FOCUS OF THE KOREAN WAR AND CURRENTLY RUNS SOUTH OF THE DEMILITARISED ZONE... "**

I should have guessed. The first clues that South Korea operates on a unique set of rules came even before I'd landed in Seoul. The customs form stated that anyone importing deer antlers or counterfeit banknotes must declare these on arrival.

I was rather disappointed not to be carrying anything among their long list of restricted items. I'd have loved to open a suitcase full of forged dollars with a triumphant flourish, but apart from ice axe and crampons my luggage was really rather conventional.

Geographically squeezed out on a limb between their powerful neighbours of China and Japan, Koreans have evolved their own way of doing things. In the eyes of the world the peninsula remains associated with the Korean War, and an uneasy stand-off

between North and South has prevailed for the last 50 years. This should not deter the potential visitor, however; there are some signs of a thawing in the relationship, and it's unlikely that your trekking holiday will be spoilt by sudden hostilities.

Only a little bigger than Ireland, Korea is a mountainous country boasting numerous National Parks, many with peaks up to 1500m. It's possible to reach anywhere in a matter of hours, so in a week or two you can get round many of Asia's most beautiful and least publicised hills, and enjoy excellent day walks on a network of well-marked trails. Longer routes are also possible during the summer months when the mountain huts are open.

Korea is known as The Land of the Morning Calm, although you have to get away from the rush-hour traffic of downtown Seoul for that to ring true. I was relieved to escape the capital for the relative tranquillity of the Korean Lake District. Out on the frozen lakes, huddles of locals sat staring intently into small holes. Ice fishing requires a lot of patience and a well-insulated bum. Those not occupied with catching dinner were skating and sledging.

The calm didn't last. I crossed the infamous 38th Parallel without incident, to discover that the northern part of South Korea is one of the most heavily fortified places on the planet. The landscape was strewn with dozens of army camps, the roads were choked with military convoys and columns of soldiers marching to some classified destination. Formations of helicopters kept an eye on my progress as I passed through roadblocks, saluted through junctions by diminutive military police in braided uniforms.

My first goal was Sorak-san in the north-east of Korea, which

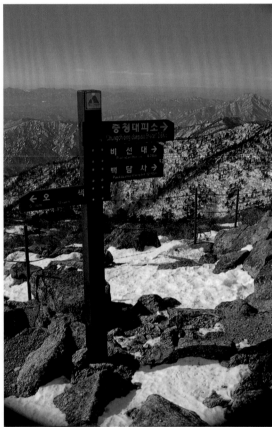

Signpost on the summit of Taech'ongbong (1708m).

A monk at Naksansa Temple

according to the tourist brochure is the 'jewel in the crown' of the Korean National Parks. Certainly it is spectacular; an extensive massif of wooded hills interspersed with rock outcrops and steep ravines. The main summit is Taech'ongbong (1708m), and on a clear day it may allow you an unauthorised peek into the North, 50km further along the coast.

With the warden sitting on the floor of the hut, I managed to avoid the entrance fee to the National Park and set off up the steep climb through snow-laden forests. Overhead a squirrel scurried through the branches dropping missiles on unwary walkers. Meanwhile a helicopter swept across the hillsides looking for foreign spies. I hid under a tree.

A three hour grind led to the windy Taech'ongbong summit, above the treeline. Some enormous communication golf balls (no doubt spying on the North, who were spying right back at them) dominated a subsidiary top. Ahead on the ridge was a large wooden lodge, or was it a cunningly disguised secret weapons facility? Anyway, being winter, it was closed, and I seemed to have Sorak-san to myself.

Blue sky and sunshine combined with plastered snow conditions for a perfect day. I followed an undulating ridge through the pinewoods for 7km without meeting anyone. It was only on the descent that I bumped into Mr Kim. I was not surprised – rough estimates indicate that at least 25 per cent of the population has the name Kim. This means you can accost someone in the high street with a cheery "Mr Kim, I presume?!" and have a one-in-four chance of being right.

To the south of Sorak-san is Osaek Hot Springs, a good spot to recover from the day's exertions. I also indulged in a plate of kimchee, Korean cabbage in a spicy sauce which comes with every meal whether you want it or not. By local standards this is conventional fare. For the discerning palate one popular delicacy is dog, which can be a bit difficult for Westerners to stomach. Dog-owners should keep their pooches firmly on a lead to avoid any confusion over dinner arrangements.

Overnight I stayed in a *yogwan*, one of the simple motels found all over the country. The woman at the desk confirmed they had rooms then asked, if I wanted a bed. Not such a silly question in Korea, where the locals prefer to sleep on the floor, one way to enjoy the underfloor heating which comes as standard. Dim red lighting and frilly bedcovers hint at the yogwans' main patronage, but 'love hotels' are also quite acceptable for those seeking nothing more than a night's sleep.

On the northern side of Sorak-san, I stopped at the village of Sorak-dong, which boasts a tourist cable car to a nearby summit. The area is scattered with granite pinnacles and large waterfalls which become frozen cascades in the winter months. Enterprising locals were renting out strap-on 'ice cleats', mini crampons to prevent embarrassing tumbles on the frozen trails.

Moving on, I stopped at an expressway service station reminiscent of an average day on Cairn Gorm, snow blasting horizontally across the car park. A major expedition was needed just to reach the sanctuary of the coffee counter. Inside, the facilities included a drum kit and a weights bench, novel ways for drivers to unwind from the stress of the wheel. Outside, a column of 200 soldiers marched through the storm, committed to the national cause – defence; I sped on before I could be conscripted.

At Odae-san the entrance charge seemed a bit steep, but with a few blank looks Mr Kim let me in for free. Behaving like an ignorant foreigner can often pay dividends. In any case getting to grips with the local language was beyond me, given that Korean seems to be punctuated by the most peculiar sounds. These can variously resemble an electric toothbrush, the onset of a violent sneeze, or a bronchitic sheep. Such outbursts come as a shock to the casual listener, and are far from easy to imitate.

A scenic drive up a steep valley led to the Park HQ at Sangwonsa Temple, where I kitted up for a walk as the weather improved. Other groups were out and about near the lower temples, but higher up, the hills were quiet save for a few locals telling me the trail was closed. However I found that if you didn't mind flailing through the occasional snowdrift then it was most definitely open. I completed a fine traverse along the ridge between the two highest summits, Pirobong (1563m) and Sangwangbong (1493m), descending in the calm of the late afternoon as the sun set.

Above the town of Wonju I found the Chiak-san National Park. The ever-present Mr Kim manned the ticket office, demanding 1100 Won for a walk in the snow. There seemed to be nobody else around so I must have constituted his day's takings.

Several hours' ascent up a wooded ravine brought me to the summit ridge and the Sangdonsa Temple. I left my boots in the hall and sat on the floor, since – as with beds – Korea has a dire shortage of chairs. Maybe the IMF confiscated large quantities of Korean furniture as collateral during the recent Asian economic crisis. The locals glanced up briefly then returned to their newspapers. They certainly seemed unfazed by a foreigner walking in off their mountain top.

They gave me some coffee but refused my proffered money. Apparently paying for something in a Korean temple would be a big insult. However by then it was too late: I'd already politely declined their offer of a meal which would also have been free. Darn! Thus it was shown that the maxim 'no such thing as a free lunch' does not necessarily apply – at least on top of this mountain.

## Fact file

### GETTING THERE
There are direct flights between London and Seoul using Korean Air. Routing options through Hong Kong (Cathay Pacific, BA), Bangkok (Thai International), Amsterdam (KLM) and Frankfurt (Lufthansa) etc. are also feasible.
British nationals do not need a visa for Korea.

### GETTING AROUND
Korea is a small country with an excellent road and rail network. Travel on public transport is relatively cheap and very efficient. Hitchhiking is possible in rural areas. To get the most out of your time here, hire a car at the airport.

### ACCOMMODATION
Comfortable *yogwan* / motel accommodation is available everywhere. It's possible to haggle over prices. Campsites and mountain huts are open in the summer. Wild camping is discouraged.

### NATIONAL PARKS
There are dozens of National Parks scattered around the country, the majority concentrated in the north and east. They have information boards at the entrances, and paths are well signed. Hills are often wooded right up to the summits so sticking to the trail may be the only option.
The Parks can be very popular with Korean hikers, particularly on weekends and public holidays.

### MAPS AND INFORMATION
*The Lonely Planet Guide to South Korea* is a good introduction to the country and culture. It is possible to buy good quality maps in bookshops in Seoul, Pusan and other major cities. Information is normally displayed at each National Park HQ, and they may have maps available for purchase, although you cannot rely on this.
The writer found an excellent book in a Korean bookshop entitled *Mountaineering Guide Maps in Korea* (ISBN 89-390-0013-7) which covers all the National Parks and so on at around 1:50,000 scale. It also gives fairly realistic walking times for the trails.
See also Michael Kelsey's *Climbers' and Hikers' Guide to the World's Mountains*, available from Cordee – tel. (0116) 254 3579.

After the short plod up to the summit of Namdaebong (1188m) I slithered off down the track. A few locals were puffing up the trail, all smartly turned out. Koreans are undoubtedly the world's best-dressed hikers. Not for them army surplus anoraks or tatty cast-off corduroys. Oh no, it has to be knee-high decorated red socks, a bright purple waistcoat, and a chic piece of yellow headgear to top off the ensemble. And as for equipment; well, it's not surprising to see ice axes and ropes being carried on summer rambles through the woods.

Heading back to Seoul, I detoured to the DMZ. The Demilitarised Zone dividing the two Koreas has developed into a bizarre tourist attraction, visitors coming to gawp at one of the world's longest stalemates. Along a 270km line the two sides have been peering at each other through barbed wire for almost 50 years. At the truce village of Pammunjom you can come face to face with real live North Korean soldiers.

Each country plays music and propaganda at the enemy across the divide. Huge signboards display their respective points of view, a face-off rather like a 70's television commercial. (We washed one half of the country in communism and the other half in a traditional brand of capitalism…)

So if the split-personality of this country appeals to you, just remember a couple of things: don't take your dog, and leave the deer antlers at home.

# THE ROAD TO SALVATION?

FOR COUNTLESS CENTURIES, THE WORLD'S FAITHFUL HAVE MADE PILGRIMAGES. JASPER WINN TOOK UP HIS STAFF AND STRODE FORTH IN THEIR FOOTSTEPS.

Photographs **Jasper Winn**

'Clouds and water': the shrine and temple above Pushkar Lake, India.

became a pilgrim by accident. Or is it just that 'we're all pilgrims on the journey of life… strangers wandering stranger roads… lost in time, salvation bound'? No, no! Hang on, that's a reject Led Zeppelin lyric, surely.

So, by accident? Well, a long time ago, I was gallivanting around Celtic festivals in Spain's north-west province of Galicia, with a Dutch friend. We finally ran out of fiestas in Vigo. So, talking over a bottle of wine and a bowl of cockles apiece in a cheap restaurant, we came up with the idea of walking to Santiago de Compostela to pass the time. "It's only about a hundred miles with a few detours to catch some Bronze Age rock engravings," I reckoned. "Five days across the hills."

Carla added a gloss of religiosity to the proceedings: "We can be pilgrims – carry scallop shells, and walking sticks and… and…" She paused. "…and a flask of wine," I finished off. We'd both rather run out of pious inspiration at that point. We did know that, since medieval times, the roads to Santiago had been one of Christendom's four great pilgrimage routes, along with those to Jerusalem, Rome and Cologne. Knew, too, that the Camino de Santiago, running across the north of Spain, still carried thousands of modern pilgrims each year from all over Europe, and that the old tracks, the hospices, the holy places continued to function as they had for centuries. But we were taking the 'Portuguese road' up from the south, and few pilgrims walked the track in modern times.

First, we required essential *peregrino's* kit. Walter Raleigh summed up what we needed in an allegorical verse: 'Give me my scallop-shell of quiet. My staff of faith to walk upon, My scrip of joy, immortal diet. My bottle of Salvation, My gown of glory (hope's true gage), And then I'll take my pilgrimage.' So there you have it. A walking stick, a Karrimor 'scrip' (pouch) to carry your gear in, a water bottle and a Gore-Tex anorak-of-glory, and you're pretty much straight out of Chaucer.

Stepping past the bodies bronzing on a nudist beach, we waded into the sea to dredge up a couple of small scallop shells. And then set off north-east. Even as faux pilgrims, on this long-forgotten *camino portugués* we were a novelty. Our scallop shells dangling from our staves, acted like ecclesiastical credit cards. Every few miles men and women forking hay in the fields hailed us. "*Oiga! Peregrinos! Para! Toma un vino,*" they called. We were urged, forced even, to sit in the shade of vines and guzzle bottles of soft, new wine. The talk was of saving the hay and of the wonders of Santiago. Home-made sausages, more wine, and fruit were pressed on us as parting gifts. And this, day after day. While at nights we slept under the stars in the lee of haystacks, or spread our bags high in the hills and joked about Galicia's wolves.

On the camino portugués we were treated with a reverence totally unwarranted by our tangled hair, dusty boots and ragbag clothes. However inappropriate it was to vest their hopes in us, it seemed that, as pilgrims, our mere

Support staff on the Portuguese road to Santiago de Compostela.

'Soft' weather during the three-day pilgrimage at Lough Derg.

## "From one angle we look like hill-walkers. From another, like monks cowled and hooded…"

passing bestowed some kind of blessing on these kind, hard-working people. We found ourselves, despite scepticism, being drawn into the magic of following a pilgrimage route, of being anointed by its history. We became quieter, spent hours lost in thought, were happy in each other's company. Buzzards soared overhead. The vineyards around us had three-dimensional richness as if stacked like green boxes against the hillsides. Walking beside us were the ghosts of the English and Irish pilgrims who had come this way hundreds of years before, after taking ship to Vigo and Pontevedra.

Our entrance into Santiago came as a shock. A sudden turn among the fields, up a lane and we were in the centre, buffeted by throngs of pilgrims from the busy Jacobean route. In the Plaza de Obradoiro scallop-pendanted wanderers piled rucksacks high and raised botas of wine higher. A single-legged man on crutches, his one boot sole worn through, hopped around, ecstatic with achievement. Somebody strummed a guitar. French, German, Czech, English and ten other languages mingled. Darkness fell and the façade of the cathedral exploded with fireworks. That night we slept under a roof for the first time in a week. But the city felt hot and cramped, and it was too noisy, and too exciting. Perhaps we just hadn't travelled far enough, but it seemed that we had arrived too soon, that our feet had out-walked our souls. We headed back to the hills.

But this small, chance pilgrimage pulled a different world into focus. On future trips I began to see every country as etched by many thousands of years of pilgrimage. My eyes became sensitised to the crosses, the scallop shells, the rags tied to trees, the cups at springs that hinted at spiritual walks around the world. My nose

could smell the incense or rum or charcoal smoke that so often announced the coming together of humans to walk. I began to hear more bells and singing and chanting in the world. Hear more measured, determined footsteps.

I saw crutches, hundreds of them, pinned to the walls of the shrine of the Black Madonna near Krakow in Poland. Joined a line of Asturians hauling a marriage bed to the top of the mountains to bless a wedding. Walked saints' roads in Dingle, Wales, Spain and France; followed paths to gurus in India, and climbed to the temple above Pushkar with solemn Hindu pilgrims at dawn.

I joined a three-day pilgrimage – 'the oldest and the toughest' in Christianity on the island of St Patrick's purgatory – a 'holy Alcatraz' – in Lough Derg, where we walked around penitential beds in our bare feet for hours on end, kneeling and shuffling. One night was spent in a sleepless vigil in the basilica, and we 'fasted' on a single meal of dry toast and tea each day. Even in so restricted an area it was our constant barefoot perambulations that gave us our status as pilgrims. In the sleeting rain we all wore cheap anoraks and cagoules. From one angle we look like hill-walkers. From another, like monks cowled and hooded.

Whatever my own beliefs, I began to believe more in other people's beliefs when experienced through the nuts and bolts of these pilgrimages. The *santería* altars in Cuba with rum and cigars and tiny metal symbols to flatter the Orishas; the Venezuelan pathside shrines to voodoo gods and goddesses; the stark crucifixes in the remotest forests of Bavaria, Bohemia and Poland; the thorn tree atop a Scythian burial mound, on the Iran-Turkmenistan border, with scraps of material tied to its branches; a woman shuffling on her bloodied knees to the Basilica of

Asturian marriage bed gets the fertility treatment.

Guadaloupe in Mexico City.

On pilgrimages the past and the present came closer than I'd ever experienced. It was as if I was a stylus following the grooves recorded in the vinyl of the landscape ages before, and was now able to replay the past footsteps taken by others with my own doubter's paces. Within every religion there was the unshakeable tradition of the slow, long walk in company to a place of significance. Islam, Christianity, animism, paganism, Hinduism, Buddhism – all shared a belief, even when not articulated, in salvation and goodness through the measure of the footfall.

In medieval England there were some 70 places of pilgrimage, from tiny holy wells and stone crosses to Glastonbury Tor, the Walsingham Virgin and Canterbury Cathedral. The *Canterbury Tales* gives many clues as to the attraction of pilgrimages, not only in the Middle Ages but nowadays as well. Company, entertainment, travel and a sense of holiday. In one package.

The jolly, gap-toothed Wife of Bath, one of Chaucer's 29 pilgrims setting off from the Tabard Inn,

exemplifies a medieval mania for peregrination as strong as the modern urge for foreign holidays. She 'had thrice been to Jerusalem, seen many strange rivers and passed over them; she'd been to Rome and to Boulogne, St James of Compostela and Cologne, And she was skilled in wandering by the way.'

The *Canterbury Tales* are a world away from modern England, as I found out when, three years ago, I set off at midnight on Christmas Eve from Winchester Cathedral to start a series of walks that would eventually carry me the 150 miles or so to Canterbury Cathedral. Quite apart from the sheer lunacy of setting off in the middle of winter, it was more the feeling of being at odds with the world I was travelling through that turned the trip into a genuine penance. There was none of the company, the story-telling, the quaffing of ale in inns. And there was little spiritual reward either.

Rather, I trudged across a rain-soaked land, bivouacked in waterlogged woods, ate bread and cheese for Christmas dinner. It wasn't much fun and, to confess, I still have the last third of the trip to complete. It's not top of any 'must-do' list.

But maybe I'm just lacking in motivation. For the medieval pilgrim there was the very real feeling that visiting one of the great pilgrimage sites had a direct influence on your afterlife – that you could expurgate sins and elevate yourself to heaven or at least pick up a 'get-out-of-hell-free' card by a bit of trampsing around England or Europe. Believe that and, suddenly, taking your scrip and scallop shell on the road becomes an imperative.

# "...pick up a 'get-out-of-hell-free' card by a bit of trampsing around England or Europe"

Guru in the Indian temple at Sleemanabad.

Pilgrims en route to Zaouia Ahansal, Morocco.

A Moroccan pilgrims' tree adorned with lucky knots.

Phallic symbols at a pilgrimage shrine in northern Iran.

If the Pilgrims' Road to Canterbury can be a lonesome enough walk in modern times, Chaucer's old spirit is alive in other countries. Zigzagging around the Atlas Mountains by mule and on foot for one eight-month period meant that I often fell in with bands of Islamic pilgrims. All the 'Canterbury' characters were there: merchants, money lenders, imams, the 'Wife of Casablanca', millers, carpet weavers, troupes of travelling acrobats.

I was drawn into the current of one group – some on donkeys or mules, most on foot – flowing through the High Central Atlas to the shrine of Sidi Said Ahansal. There was a palpable sense of arrival as we reached the remote valley. Prayers were chanted around the saint's tomb, and a ram was killed and cooked. The feasting continued late into the night. But above us, on the summit of Mount Azurki, there was evidence of another kind of pilgrimage, and an altogether older tradition. Barren women, petitioning older animist gods for fertility, climbed up to the peak to sacrifice an animal and leave something of themselves as an offering. I had scrambled to the top only a few days earlier and found an enamelling of dried blood on a rock, and strips torn from a woman's petticoat.

Pilgrimages are about a joining together of people around a common belief. Any belief. Whatever. That Saint James' bones really are in Compostela having arrived there on a stone boat; that Slovenians dressed up as kurunti, with shaggy fur robes, spiked clubs, and horned and devil-tongued masks can really drive away the winter as they jog trot around their snowy landscape; that the carrying of different villages' statues of the Virgin deep into the countryside on oxen carts accompanied by explosions of flamenco and decorated horses and feasting will really bring prosperity to those Andalucian villages. But, behind them all, perhaps the real reward is in the walking.

Kurunti, chasing away winter in Slovenia.

Buddha's last words to his disciples were "Walk on." Sufis practise *siyahat* – the 'repetition of walking' – to loosen their dependence on the material world. The word for a Zen monk in Chinese is *yun shui*, meaning 'clouds and water' and signifying their freedom to move throughout the country. Pascal in his *Pensées* quoth, "Out nature lies in movement; complete calm is death."

But you might also heed an older warning to pilgrims: *Qui multum peregrinatur raro sanctificantur* – 'He who makes many pilgrimages is rarely holy.' Or, perhaps, ponder the words of a hard-working woman I met in the west of Ireland. On being told by the friend introducing us that I was "a mighty man for walking," the battleaxe looked me up and down and snorted, "Is that so now?" She turned away dismissively. "Well, I'd have little enough respect for any man with blisters on his feet and no blisters on his hands."

# HIGHLANDS IN

STIR-CRAZY FROM TOO MUCH LAZING BY THE POOL,
TOM HUTTON HEADS FOR THE HILLS IN THE BEACH
HOLIDAY PARADISE OF THE DOMINICAN REPUBLIC.

Photography **Tom Hutton**

Definitely worth getting out of bed for:
Pico Duarte's summit sunrise.

# THE SUN

I took another look at my watch and sighed irritably at the information on the dial; I'd lasted for three whole days. Okay, it was 48 hours more than the folks back home had suggested but there was no way I could deny it any more; I was bored and restless.

I won't let the sun go down on me.
Oh, all right then..

Kids will be kids, wherever they are in the world.

It had started well enough – the temperature was in the 30s, I had a beautiful condo to myself and a swimming pool and well-stocked bar within arm's reach. But I just couldn't shake off that mountain itch. No matter how hard I tried, slapping on suncream, sipping endless pina coladas and ploughing through a never-ending pile of paperbacks was clearly never going to be my thing.

So I sniffed out the island guide that I'd been trying so hard to ignore. Scanning the index frantically, my eyes came to rest on three words – The Central Highlands. I checked the reference – these were claiming to be the highest peaks in the Caribbean. I read on and felt a tinge of excitement course through my veins – Pico Duarte, first climbed in 1944, was 3175m (yes, metres not feet!). That was as high as some of the better-known mountains of the Alps. If it wasn't so close to the equator, it'd be glaciated! I patted myself squarely on my sunburnt back for remembering to bring a small selection of outdoor kit – I had an adventure to organise.

We met at 7am. Not early by mountain climbing standards, but early for these parts. 'We' were Mike, an instantly likeable, tall Canadian was to be our guide for the next few days; Beat and Regula – a pretty sporty Swiss couple who, like me, had had enough of watching their skin crinkle up in a swimming pool; and myself. Mike, who worked for the local adventure tour specialists, Iguana Mama, briefed us on the itinerary over breakfast, and then, with the formalities over, we loaded rucksacks into the van and set off.

As we passed the last few shacks on the outskirts of the tiny town of Cabarete, I began to feel alive again. We climbed away from the coast and crossed the Cordillera Septentrional mountain range before dropping steeply into the lush and fertile Cibao Valley. Our first stop, Mocca, was a bustling town with an equally bustling market where we purchased provisions to keep us going for the next few days.

Mike had gone to great lengths to explain the emphasis that Iguana Mama puts on supporting the local community and showing visitors the true Dominican culture. Not only had we procured our food as close to the mountains as we could, but we were also to be spending our first evening on the trail with a typical Dominican family.

We bounced into La Cienaga at around 5pm, having covered the last few miles by dirt road. The van ground to a halt and, before the dust had even had a chance to settle, we were mobbed by children in varying states of undress.

We hauled our kit into the National Park office where we were introduced to Francisco, a park ranger and our host for the evening. We followed Francisco back to his home, a collection of ramshackle huts that were absolutely immaculate inside, and met his wife Celia and his eldest son, Willie, who was to be one of our guides on the trip up the mountain. Celia showed us around her home with the beaming pride of any mother who'd spent the day cleaning and preparing for visitors, and then produced a steaming cup of locally ground coffee. As we drank, others appeared: Victor, the youngest son, was followed by an endless stream of visitors, some of whom I took to be related; others, my almost non-existent Spanish told me, were just friends, curious to meet the *gringos*.

Top right: Island life, Dominican Republic-style.
Bottom left: You can put the headtorch away now!
Bottom right: Above Jarobacoa.

I BEGAN TO EXPERIENCE A FAMILIAR SENSATION
WHICH HAD BEEN A STRANGER FOR A WHILE:
THE COLD – WE WERE 1100M ABOVE SEA LEVEL

Get to the top or bust!

No matter how much I travel and how many beautiful landscapes I'm lucky enough to gaze upon, nothing moves me quite as much as spending time with different people who, occasionally, seem to come not so much from different countries and cultures but from different worlds. We wandered around the village, drinking in the sights and sounds: it was Friday night and many of the local men had gathered outside a small bar, playing dominoes and chatting in the way that people do in bars all over the planet. Down by the river, which acts as the main water source for the village, a group of teenage kids had organised a boxing match. With one glove each, guys and girls alike took turn to swing punches at their friends, the gathered crowd forming an ever-moving ring.

We ate dinner, drank more local coffee and I began to experience

## Fact file

### WHAT TO TAKE
The days are hot and humid so shorts and a good wicking top are must-haves. Night temparatures fall below freezing in the mountains so a thick fleece and Gore-Tex (or similar) are necessary. It's worth noting that if it decides to rain, it *really* rains, so waterproof trousers are also useful. A cap to keep the sun off is essential, as are gloves and a warm hat for camp and the early morning starts. Three-season walking boots would make the most sensible footwear, as the going is fairly rough in places. A 30-litre daysack is useful to carry personal kit in, but a holdall is much easier to load onto the donkeys. For the nights in the cabins, I used a 3-season sleeping bag and a headtorch.

**Tom's kit list** Lowe Alpine Dryflo and Helly Hansen Lifa base layers, Mountain Hardwear shorts, Berghaus fleece trousers, Lowe Alpine Air Attack fleece, Lowe Alpine Mountain Guide jacket, The North Face Nuptse down jacket, Sprayway waterproof trousers, Scarpa SL boots, Karrimor Hot Route 50-litre rucksack.

### LOOKING FOR ADVENTURE
Although there are a number of operators offering adventure excursions from Cabarete, a lot of it is aimed at the typical tourist. The biggest and best for more experienced outdoor lovers is Iguana Mama – tel. (001) 809 571 0908 www.iguanamama.com The guides are knowledgeable and speak excellent English. I was particularly impressed with the responsible and ethical approach they take to both the native Dominicans and the environment. Visitors wishing to climb Pico Duarte are always accompanied by National Park guides.

### WHERE TO STAY
Cabarete has a huge selection of hotels for all budgets. Try Residencia Dominicana – tel. (001) 809 571 0890 e-mail resdom@hispaniola.com for low-cost but comfortable rooms or, for a few $$ more, The Windsurf Resort – tel. (001) 809 571 0718 e-mail windsurf@codetel.net.do Check out www.hispaniola.com/Cabarete for more details and on-line booking.

### GETTING THERE
The nearest airport is Puerto Plata, which is a £15 taxi ride from Cabarete. Many tour operators run flights from the main UK airports. For low-cost deals take a look at Teletext or try any budget flight specialist.

### MONEY
The local currency is Dominican pesos but the US dollar still speaks volumes. It's possible to change sterling in the larger conurbations but I found it easier and more convenient to carry a supply of dollars too.

### WHEN TO GO
The climate is pretty steady from December-September but it gets hot in the summer months (June-September). Avoid October and November unless you want to witness torrential rain and the tail end of a few hurricanes! Early spring is probably best for walking.

### BACKGROUND READING
*The Rough Guide to the Dominican Republic & Haiti*, pb Rough Guides

another familiar sensation which had been a stranger for a while: the cold – we were 1100m above sea level. As the evening drew to a close, we said our thanks and goodnights and I retired to a warm sleeping bag on the floor of the National Park office.

We awoke at sunrise to the sound of cocks crowing. The Dominicans keep and adore cockerels in the same way as the British do dogs. Willie, now accompanied by a friend, loaded our food and a few gallons of water onto two fairly fed-up-looking donkeys and we departed at a steady pace. I have to admit that I was against the idea of climbing the mountain supported by donkeys. However, Mike, who had been suffering with a long-term knee problem, had been known to need a lift down on occasions; and there was absolutely no way our Dominican guides were going to walk with heavy packs. I reassured myself that I wasn't getting soft; I still had to walk 20km and climb 2000m, and reluctantly let the donkeys carry some water and my sleeping bag.

The walking started easily; we ambled along the riverbank for 4km to the Los Tablones cabin, where we stopped for a drink by a rickety old bridge. This was to be the last real water we'd see for two days, hence the need for the donkeys to carry our supply. Then, with the warmup over, we started climbing. The track was easy enough to follow; the relentless West Indian rain had cut it into a trench in places, deep enough to make a clay-sided bobsleigh run, but some sections were incredibly steep and we were reduced almost to a crawling pace at times. The trees provided valuable shade from the ever-strengthening sun but I resented them a little for blocking out much of the view.

Eventually we broke into a huge clearing and were met with stunning views over the other high mountains of the Cordillera Central. It's difficult to imagine a more green and fertile place. The mountains, which stretched as far as the eye could see, were blanketed with an almost continuous covering of pine trees. The valley floors, used mainly for grazing cattle and sheep, were a luminescent green, peppered with the lanky outlines of majestic king palms, swaying in the breeze. The silence only broken by bird calls.

We stopped frequently, mainly to drink, as the heat was becoming intense, and crossed the 2000m contour line just after lunch. We climbed, mainly in the open, for a further 3 hours and then, at just short of 2700m, we started to descend. We dropped almost 200 sacred metres during the next 40 minutes yet were rewarded with the welcoming site of La Comparticion, a small cabin 650m short of the summit. We would rest here, eat dinner and get an early night. Tomorrow we'd set off at 4.30 in order to reach the top by sunrise. It had been a long day and I didn't need much rocking.

Odd though it may seem, I take my down jacket everywhere with me, even the West Indies! The next morning, as I stepped out of the cabin onto the frost-covered grass of the clearing, I congratulated myself on my foresight. It was freezing with a capital F. Apparently, a lot of the locals climb the mountain purely to find out what it's like to be cold!

We left most of our kit at the camp, where the guides still slept soundly and the donkeys munched their way through anything that looked edible, and set off towards the summit. A full moon did a good job of illuminating our way, and our headtorches did little but hold our hats in place.

For over an hour we climbed through the forest, the only sound being that of our feet crunching through the frosty grass. Then, without any warning, the trees ended. Directly ahead and no more than 50 metres away was a bold rocky outcrop, crowned with flags, crosses and a small, but impressive, statue.

We scrambled the last few metres, still in the dark, and regrouped on the top. Sunrise was still some way off but the

The Dawn Patrol heads down the mountain.

eastern sky was already beginning to glow a pearly pink that seemed to get brighter by the second. The full moon, which had guided us so confidently from the cabin, appeared to be shrinking away from the coming day and far, far below, the Dominican lowlands lay sleeping, shrouded in cloud.

Slowly but surely, a flaming red orb edged its way above the cloud to cast light and warmth on our huddled group. Few things can be as timeless as a sunrise and no matter how many I see, I still take something special from the re-emergence of the mightiest energy source of them all. It's easy to see how our ancestors placed so much significance on this magical moment.

Today, however, had been different; I'd witnessed the spectacle from the summit of Pico Duarte – the highest point in the whole of the Caribbean.

It's clearly Jasper's turn to make the tea (again).

# TWO IN THE BUSH

KEEN TO ACQUAINT HIMSELF WITH THE 'REAL' AUSTRALIA, JASPER WINN ABANDONS THE ART OF FREMANTLE FOR THE HEART OF THE OUTBACK.

Photography **Jasper Winn**

Before I'd ever visited Australia I knew all about the outback from watching Skippy the Bush Kangaroo every week as a seven-year-old, and learning an annoying ditty about kookaburras being 'merry little kings of the bush' in school at about the same age. So, when I actually pitched up in Western Australia three decades later, I just knew that the outback was populated by marsupials who could tell you with a wrinkle of their nose and a 'kissy kissy' sound that two small boys had fallen down a mine shaft. And I knew, too, that the whole Australia experience was going to be soundtracked by plunking banjos and overgrown kingfishers chortling in merry laughter.

I was barely off the plane in Perth before I'd plucked a eucalyptus leaf from the nearest gum tree so I too could make that haunting, inverted wolf-whistle that heralded Skippy's adventures. Well, blow as I might, I couldn't. And so, somewhat peeved, I spent the next two months turning my back on the bush and, instead, running an art gallery in the heart of funky Fremantle, and making a television documentary about rodeo riders in the far-from-funky small towns to the south. But the call of the bush was still there. There was bush all over the place. It crept like dry rot into the very heart of the city. Cockatoos and kangaroos flew and bounded around Perth's parks, or ended up as road kill on suburban highways. And Australia's urban majority regularly got lost in the bush and appeared in the local newspapers, not for winning a golf tournament or hosting a Rotary Club dinner, but by dying.

I decided to meet the bush on its own terms. A section of the 964km long Bibbulmun Track walking trail, that ran from the edge of Perth to Albany far down in the south, had just been rerouted and upgraded, providing a pleasant, three-day, 55km hike from the city's suburbs down to the Brookton Highway. I saw myself as a jolly swagman, billy over the fire, hunks of mutton and bottles of red wine pulled from my rucksack, waltzing my Matilda through the gum trees.

Except that I ended up waltzing Heidi. She was a Dutch, globe-trotting waitress working in my local café. Seeing me flapping a map around one morning, she deduced I was going walking. "Can I come too?" she asked. Tough question. I like walking alone. But then again I figured that two of us sharing a bottle of Jacob's Creek and a steak or two around the campfire would be fun as well. "Yeah, sure." "But can I do the food buying?" she added. "I'm a bit fussy about what I eat." I put in a request for meat dripping blood and strong red wine, and we arranged to leave the next morning.

We puttered to the edge of Kalamunda suburb in Heidi's combi van.

It was awesome how quickly the supermarkets and mown lawns dropped off into nothing but red dirt, eucalyptus trees and venomous snakes.

The bush is like a pleasant Mediterranean park expanded to such cosmic proportions that a bit of misnavigation (for which I am famed in five continents) can lead you into light years of 'dreaming' and an unpleasant Burke and Wills-style death in the middle of nowhere.

Wine and lunch en route to the trail head had perhaps taken a little longer than we thought. And by the time we'd faffed around with our packs and then disinfected our boots so we didn't trample 'dieback' – the botanical equivalent of foot-and-mouth – into the virgin outback, it was already late afternoon. We walked a mere 3km before reaching Ball Creek campsite. Heidi threw her rucksack down and settled herself comfortably in the last rays of the sun. I come from a school of walking that demands double figures and at least 2 as the first digit when it comes to daily mileage. But I was on my best behaviour, and she had a point.

"Right-i-oh!" I agreed, lighting a fire. "I'll unpack the food." Heidi gestured at her pack: "It's in the top, in a bag." Indeed it was. In a small, very small, bag. Inside was some rice, two avocados, six oranges, a pound of muesli, and some rabbit foody bits. Which had to last us three days. "I thought the walk would be a chance to eat well," Heidi told me brightly. "You know – naturally." I'd brought no more than a packet of salted seaweed and a pound of coffee beans. I felt hungry already.

To hide my disappointment I sloped off into the bush. It was almost dark, and the shadows were filled with Australia's native fauna busy stuffing their offspring into pouches and chewing on leaves or on each other according to taste. It's not generally known that after Lewis Carroll wrote Jabberwocky he had lots of silly names for equally silly animals left over. He sold the names to the Western Australian Tourist Board who then subcontracted God to come up with the animals to fit the names. Which is why this part of the world not only has wambengers, quokkas, woylies, quolls, quendas and many other weird-sounding examples of fauna, but also why a bilby, for example, looks exactly as you'd expect a bilby to look. Or would have looked like if I could have seen one. There were rustlings and scufflings and squeaks in the gloom, and an eruption of birdsong in the treetops above. Ears took over from eyes, aromas percolated from the earth and even the breeze had a taste. As I walked back into the firelight there was a pot of rice bubbling on the embers. And a plate of avocado slices. Heidi was humming happily.

We set off early the next morning. Because I'd come to Oz to work, I was low on walking gear. So I strode the track bracketed by those two icons of Australian life – the Akubra hat and Blunstone work boots. I couldn't have looked more Australian if I'd been Rolf Harris in an Emu costume. Though I could have been more comfortable, and less peckish. I was chewing on coffee beans for their food content. With two more days to go and food already running low, I was thinking in terms of 'bush tucker'. Skippy the kebabbed kangaroo with pepper sauce, perhaps. Or witchetty grubs, which a friend who ran a 'indigenous foods' restaurant had told me tasted "just like Camembert in a condom".

It's always difficult walking with somebody you don't know. And interesting. Different stride lengths; a tendency to burst into song or fall deeply silent; a need to carry a stick and slash at overhanging fronds, or chew on grass stalks. All are individual choices and they're as potentially divisive as religious beliefs, hardline politics or habitual spitting can be in a new friendship. Heidi and I, though, had been matched in heaven. Within 20 minutes without a word being said we had wandered apart, walking separately, and waiting or speeding up to meet every hour or so for a chat, a swig of water and a pinch of seaweed. It was an amicable decision – I felt closer to Heidi as we went our own ways than I have to many people I have matched stride for stride.

There can be few greater luxuries than to walk alone knowing that you have company up ahead or coming up behind whenever you want it.

The Bibbulmun was deceptive. The path had been cleared, and any doubt in the trail was decided by the snake motif on a small triangle pointing the way. We could have been in a park, except that in a half day's walking we were exactly half a day from anything that might be termed a road, a house or indeed a source of food.

Still, it was benign walking. A gentle susurration of birdsong and insect noises lulled the kilometres away. There were little bursts of activity, too. At one point I heard a wheezy whistling broken by manic muttering and chuckling in the grass jungle beside me. There was a pattering and flapping and a sextet of Baudin's cockatoos – black plumaged and with a dippy flight – fluttered into a burnt-out gum tree to laugh and swear at me. I saw my first kookaburra, too; a bandit-masked bird who dissolved into hysterical laughter at the sight of me shuffling along in a cowboy hat and glorified riding boots.

Heidi and I met up again some 18km down the trail at the Waalegh campsite. Simple, wooden, three-walled shelters are spaced along the trail at roughly 10km intervals. They're built by prison work parties, though obviously using low security prisoners, as under Western Australia's draconian penal system hard-core offenders are actually transported to Earl's Court and made to work in tele-sales. Each camp has a tank of rain water, a fire circle and a drop-pit 'thunderbox' toilet.

Waalegh was a stunner, pitched on a ridge, looking across to the Darling mountains, and high above an unfocused nimbus of treetops in the valley far below. After a minimum-water washdown, and without much in the way of food to distract us, we

"Rod who?"                    Wiggly waymark.

Heidi logs on.                    Emu tonight?

This is the bush, baby...    Sarongs without words.

Grave implications?    Sunset's trip.

sat looking into the sunset.

Heidi had, perhaps, come looking for some kind of spiritual experience on the Bibbulmun, the opposite of a steak-and-alcohol-fuelled machismo yomp.

And I'd come to agree with her. We had walked through a magical land; we both felt light and easy with it, as if we had been carried along on a song line, and the trail's Aboriginal waugal – the rainbow serpent from an ancestral dreaming – had a real resonance and meaning.

Later, in the freezing darkness, huddled together by the fire, I took out the camp log book which I'd found stored in a woylie-proof box on a shelf in the shelter. "Listen to this one," I said, holding the book so I could read by the light of the flames. "'I walked from Mundaring to this campsite and I am egsousteade...' – that's the way it's spelt – '...and my mum sease im togh an I am 7 years old and my name is Jed Berry.' And then there's another bit tagged on: 'Jed did abut 23km. I wanted to stop about 4km back but Jed said no, Mum, we can do it.'" This small entry, too, seemed to have some kind of elemental magic in it.

We talked late into the night, feeding the fire with dead wood, and letting the subject drift as it would around the flames and smoke. It got chillier still and a fog drifted out from the trees. I fell asleep next to the fire with Heidi still telling stories. Before dawn I got up to light the fire for coffee; it was icy cold and misty. We ate the last of the muesli; the last of the food and packed and set off as the sun rose over the trees. We both had work in the morning and had to cover the 30km to Brookton Highway to hitch back to the city. Heidi was soon far ahead, striding up the hills into an area of pine trees and tiny Alpine-style meadows. Leading into the gum forest that followed, she left the occasional note for me under a stone to tell me what she was thinking and how far ahead she was. She had rather charmingly taken to combining the outback and the bush into one entity she called 'bushback'.

Towards the end of the day I met the first and only person we passed on the trail in two and a bit days of walking. He was marching along with a rucksack. "Hey, are you the poofter with the girl beating you by half an hour?" he didn't say. "Your friend's up ahead of you," is what he actually said, but I can read people's minds. Heidi had in fact stopped at the Mount Dale campsite and was lounging in the sun as I walked in. I was hungry. Prowling around inside the shelter I found the usual small plastic box with the camp log book inside. And a foil-wrapped soup-stock wafer left behind by a previous walker. "Hey, look at this!" I cried jubilantly. "Do you think it's still okay to use?" Heidi looked over. "What is it? Oh, a condom. Yes, probably." My imagination immediately conjured up a hugely seductive vision of a luscious round of ripe Camembert. Brought back to real life I crumbled the stock concentrate into a mug of cold water. It was truly awful. But good.

A couple of hours later we stumbled out onto the Brookton Highway as if we were Japanese jungle warfare veterans who'd just learned that the war was over. We dumped our pack by a road sign and stuck out our thumbs. There were emu tracks, great clawed dinosaur prints, in the dirt by the side of the tarmac. I assumed they had been hitching back to town as well. I can only hope they had more luck than we did. The few cars and trucks that passed accelerated and swerved away from us when we came into view. I could see their point. I wouldn't have given me a lift. I would even have thought twice about giving Heidi a lift.

We contemplated another night in the bush. I wondered if one could kill an emu with a penknife. In desperation Heidi jumped out in front of a pickup truck which, given no choice, squealed to a halt. The driver had tattoos that started under his fingernails. "Eh, I'll give youse both a lift, but I don't normally take people in me truck – you don't know what kind of mad folk are out on roads, and I'd be bloody scared of getting some murderer type." We climbed in gratefully. To make conversation, I asked him about the gun loosely wrapped in sacking under the seat. "Eh, you know, I likes to shoot things now and again – more for sport than anything – wild boar, some rabbits, that kind of thing." It turned out our benefactor was a shearer, poacher, and all-round nice guy who took us far out of his way to drop us at a suburban Perth train station.

"You be careful now, 'cos there's some mad bastards out there." He winked, so I could clearly see the tattoo on his left eyelid. "And I'm not so sure you ain't two of them, for walking all that way in the bush." He drove off. I turned toward the nearest restaurant. "I need some tucker, Heidi." I began walking. "I want a 'Skippy burger', an outback salad and the strongest red wine civilisation can provide – and fast. It's your choice whether you want something but say 'yes' and it's my treat." For pretty much the first time on the whole trip we walked side by side.

## Fact file

### GETTING THERE
British Airways – tel. (0845) 77 333 77; www.britishairways.com run flights from Heathrow to Perth, with a refuelling stop in Singapore, making them almost direct.

### TRAVEL INFO
Contact the Australian Tourist Commission – tel. (0870) 556 1434; www.australia.com

### BIBBULMUN TRACK
The complete 964km walking trail runs from the outskirts of Perth to Albany. It's well marked, largely with shelters at regular intervals. Despite this level of management, many levels are remote and with no easy way out to get help in emergencies. Water is not sure in all parts in all seasons, and you need to carry water bottles; warm, waterproof clothing (weather can be extreme);

sun protection and ample food. If you get lost it's vital to not walk aimlessly – you are easier to find the closer you are to the path. Leave details of your itinerary with somebody responsible so if you don't reappear the alarm can be raised; equally, remember to tell that same person when you do reappear so no unnecessary searches are started.

The Kalamunda to North Bannister Map 1 Bibbulmun track map covers the section Perth to Brookton Highway in great detail.

For further Bibbulmun information try the following websites: www.calm.wa.gov.au/bibbulmun_splash.htm; www.Bibbulmuntrack.org.au

Books and maps covering the Bibbulmun Track are widely available in Western Australian bookshops and camping suppliers.

# ICE AND A SLICE OF ACTION

MILFORD TRACK, INCA TRAIL, LAUGAVEGUR: CONTINENTAL TREKKERS KNOW ALL THESE WALKS, BUT ASK A BRIT AND THE LAST ONE WILL BE A MYSTERY. SO, AFTER THE SNOW CLEARED LAST SUMMER, ROB DENMAN WENT TO FATHOM THE FROZEN MOONSCAPE THAT HOSTS ICELAND'S FINEST TREK.

Photography **Tom Bailey**

The glacier at the head of the Krossá valley.

**M**ulti-coloured, skimpy Speedos. And not an ugly beach scene, but the kitchen in our hut at Thórsmörk. It was tough to take. I know the high passes of the world are not meant to be at the pinnacle of fashion but, after a hard trek through a real wilderness, I was having enough problems preparing my own food pack without having to face my Italian friend's luminous lunchbox.

Deep in south-central Iceland the god Thor, to whom the area is dedicated, would have fallen off his Viking perch at this shameless display. However, we only had ourselves to blame, having opted for the stifling comforts of the cabin over chilly canvas accommodation.

Volcanic sand dune running and not a beach in sight.

It was our base for a three-day glimpse at the 78km Laugavegur, the finest trek north of the 60th parallel. Crammed with Europeans of every hue and tongue, except Brits, the Thórsmörk hut is four days south-west of the usual start point of Landmannalaugar, and a day north-east of trail's end at Skógar. Our plan was to sample a nearby glacier, strike out north-east along the trail for a day's trek and do the same the next day, this time south-east towards Skógar. Just enough to see if we can entice you to claim the area for British trekkers.

Others are onto it. The Laugavegur has been tipped by Lonely Planet to join the Inca Trail and Milford Track as one of the finest walks in the world..

Thórsmörk is a two and a half hour 4x4 coach drive from Reykjavik, at the head of the wooded Markarfljót valley. As the coach forded the streams on the way up, I couldn't help being reminded of the early days of motoring when someone used to wade into the rapids with a long pole, testing the depth to see if it was safe for the vehicle to follow.

We arrived at Thórsmörk in the late afternoon but, as it's just south of the Arctic circle, the sun was still high. We hiked up the valley to get a closer look at one of the glacier's fingers, which stretch down to just 200m above sea level.

From our base on the north side we crossed the churning streams that fanned across the valley bottom before we could head for higher ground. After crossing the main stream by a temporary bridge, the other rivulets involved a mastermind-like approach to make Magnus Magnusson proud. We noticed that as the days went by, in-depth analysis was replaced by faster and considerably wetter crossings.

The rock in most of the area is volcanic palogonite which is easily eroded by the harsh environment. The rugged ridges stealing away down the valleys had scree, slopes and crests that would keep Trail readers entertained for days.

# Fact file

## WHEN TO GO
July and August are best, if only because many huts are closed outside of these months. It is possible to trek during the other summer months but snow will be a serious threat.

## GETTING THERE
Icelandair flies all year from London Heathrow and Glasgow (www.icelandair. co.uk – tel. (020) 7874 1000) to Keflavik. Flight time is around 3 hours.
Go! from BA flies to Reykjavik regularly. Details from www.go-fly.com or – tel. (0870) 607 6543.

## GETTING AROUND
Keflavik is about 45 minutes from Reykjavik and a fly-bus connects with every flight. Car rental in Iceland is very expensive and all the major firms have offices at the airport. The main bus company (www.bsi.is) operates across Iceland and out to Thórsmörk and Landmannalaugar. The buses usually run early in the morning but, in line with most things in Iceland, a return to Thórsmörk is expensive.

## ACCOMMODATION
The place to stay in Reykjavik is the oldest hotel in Iceland, the Borg – tel. (00354) 551 1440.
There are also many guesthouses such as the Bundesbra with its own sauna and jacuzzi – tel. (00354) 552 6646.
Icelandair's Flughotel in Keflavik is just 10 minutes from the airport with a bus link to the terminal – tel. (00354) 421 5222.

## TREK DETAILS
Campsites in Thórsmörk and along the route cost from £5 per night, while huts cost up to £11. Along the trek most of the huts are run by the Icelandic Touring Club, Feroafelag Islands – tel. (00354) 568 2533, www.fi.is. The website is mainly in Icelandic but they are developing an English version. Make sure you book huts in advance.

## GEAR
With so many rivers to ford, gaiters are useful and, as the weather can change rapidly, you must be prepared for all conditions. Most of the huts have limited stocks available to buy but they are (you guessed it) expensive. Bring what you can from the UK. Good 3-4 season boots will cope with all the terrain and keep your feet dry.

No need to spend time navigating – search out the views instead.

The aptly-named Krossá.

The only fauna we encountered were a multitude of moths and omnipresent, wheeling seabirds. Occasionally, polar bears from nearby Greenland brave the frozen sea to walk to Iceland but they soon learn that the friendly people do not extend their welcome to bears; rather, the intruders are greeted with very unfriendly bullets.

The western edge of the valley splits into smaller canyons, all leading to the white mass of Myrdalsjökull glacier. The nearer section was stained with earth and walking across looked dicey so, rather than pitting ourselves against the boggy murk, we returned to our accommodation, which by now had turned into a hotbed of European culture. Our Italian friend was one of only a dozen nationalities and it was good to meet some Japanese. They always seem to be throwing themselves at any challenge the world has to offer with the finest kit and an unbounded sense of humour.

Next morning, as the sun glinted off the glaciers, we unexpectedly retrieved summer gear and headed north towards Emstrur hut for a taste of the main trail. This is a 6-7 hour walk and, as we were starting at the 'wrong' end, we didn't expect to encounter anyone else for a few hours. Instead, we soon met a Frenchman who had left his camp at 5am. He confirmed our observation about Britons: "I have been here for a month and you are the first British I have seen!"

As we gradually climbed, the terrain changed from grassy plain through volcanic plateau to black basalt sand, but everywhere the way was marked by rocky cairns and wooden posts. These punctuate the full length of the trek so, depending on your view on signs in the wilderness, prepare to be pleased or horrified.

The area is all part of a national park so, if you take a detailed map, unlimited choices for getting off the trail are available. The trekking and scrambling can provide spectacular views and solitude, but bear in mind that the Icelandic mountain rescue team will only be called out if someone is aware you are missing, so let a third party know your plans.

With just 270,000 people on the island, most of them living in Reykjavik, you can walk for days without finding any signs of life. Alternative entertainment being limited, if you get lost within reach of Reykjavik, hundreds of strapping locals will fight for the honour of saving you, but further afield the rescue missions tend to be more, er, intermittent.

"The polar bear? Yeah, I killed it. Bare-handed too."

Looking to the horizon the clear sky was starting to fill with disc-shaped clouds (lenticularis, we were told that evening) above the heads of the glaciers. An old Icelandic saying goes 'If the weather is bad, wait five minutes and it will get worse,' so with this in mind we turned and headed back for Thórsmörk where the heavens promptly opened.

Land of ice – but the trekking's hot.

With the rain still teeming down next morning we headed south across the valley floor towards a glacier pass called Fimmvörðuhals which leads down to Skógar. This 27km (9 hour) trek involves climbing through verdant valleys to 1116m, then out across windswept, rocky plateaux and glacial fields. It was all spectacularly beautiful.

As we climbed, the trail crossed several high ridges, sometimes over guide rails which have been added where the soft soil has suffered from wear. The trail has become a trench in many places as trekking poles, useful for preventing human joint erosion, have dug into the path's edges.

The views across Thórsmörk and along the Krossá valley showed the trail back to the Emstrur hut. Beyond, the multi-coloured volcanic region of Landmannalaugar glowed with reds, greens, yellows and blues thanks to the underlying rhyolite. The term 'moonscape' is far too frequently used for barren terrain but it's appropriate here, and NASA agrees. The area was used for acclimatisation purposes by the Apollo astronauts. And now there is talk of it being used as a backdrop for the movie *Tomb Raider*.

The descent back home took less than two hours and we arrived at our cosy hut by 7pm. The sun was still high in the sky and there was enough light left for England to lose a test match, but my legs had walked enough.

According to Jules Verne, Iceland is the gateway to the centre of the earth and as we sat in Reyjkavik the next afternoon we noticed the prices definitely seemed to be from another level. Our farewell pints cost £6.50 each so thank Thor that Iceland's greatest attraction, its vast and challenging outdoor arena, comes free.

The varied landscapes created by every geological phenomenon from hot springs to glacial ice fields make for a superb trek, and at an altitude that makes breathing an unconscious pleasure rather than a constant problem. Start saving and go and claim the trail for Britain. Just leave your dayglo Speedos behind.

# The Laugavegur Trek

Trekkers usually start at the northern point in Landmannalaugar as it's mostly downhill from there. But it can also be done from the other end, starting at either Thórsmörk or Skógar.

### DAY 1
Landmannalaugar to Hrafntinnusker
**10KM 4-5 HOURS**
**ALTITUDE CHANGE +470M**

Regarded as the hardest day, but arguably the most spectacular. The route crosses the Laugahraun lava flow and the red, green, yellow and blue of the rhyolite and volcanic terrain combine to spectacular effect. There are plenty of hot springs but treat them with care as many are very hot. The overnight hut is the only one that cannot be driven to so everything carried in has to be carried out. There are ice caves nearby if time and weather allow. Many trekkers ignore this first hut – it's covered in fog most of the time – and carry on to Alftavatn.

### DAY 2
Hrafntinnusker to Alftavatn
**11KM 4-5 HOURS**
**ALTITUDE CHANGE −490M**

The later in the season you come the harder this section becomes. There are many small peaks and passes to cross and earlier in the summer you can use snow bridges to cross some of them. Huskeroinger summit (1281m) lies just off the main trail for a taste of peak-bagging and, if the weather is clear, has lovely views over Kaldaklofsfjöll icecap. This is sometimes referred to as the ghost hut after the death of an Icelander in 1838. You may not be alone...

### DAY 3
Alftavatn to Emstrur
**16KM 6-7 HOURS**
**ALTITUDE CHANGE −40M**

This outing involves following a 4x4 track for 10km and fording various streams. It has the reputation as the least exciting part of the trek. Near the end of the day is an area of black sand that can prove difficult but, if the weather allows, the views can be enough for you to cancel your return ticket.

### DAY 4
Emstrur to Thórsmörk
**14KM 6-7 HOURS**
**ALTITUDE CHANGE −300M**

Approximately one hour into the walk the trail crosses a spectacular canyon by a narrow bridge with a rope guide. You then leave the river and descend towards Thórsmörk valley across easy terrain. One of the most treacherous points of the trek is the unbridged Throngá river – be careful. It is then less than an hour through wood and brushland to the Feroafelag Islands hut at Thórsmörk.

### DAY 5
Thórsmörk to Skógar
**27KM 9 HOURS**
**ALTITUDE CHANGE −200M**

Many finish the walk in Thórsmörk but the final section can provide another slant on Icelandic scenery. The climb to the Fimmvörðuhals pass (1116m) is initially along the top of a steep ridge but then it opens out across snowswept rock and barren ice fields. There are two huts where you can spend the night, and sunrise over the glacier is quite a sight. The descent to Skógar passes waterfalls and views across the sea before finishing on the coastal plain.

If the wind changes...! Face-pulling on the roof of the Jokhang temple, Lhasa.

# KID WITH ALTITUDE

ORGANISATIONAL NIGHTMARES, EXTRA LUGGAGE AND MAJOR HEALTH RISKS: WHY WOULD ANYONE TAKE A CHILD TREKKING IN TIBET? BECAUSE THE REWARDS ARE BOUNDLESS...

Words and photographs **Wendy Teasdill**

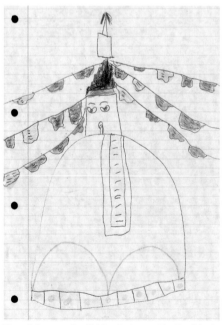

Through the eyes of a child. Iona's picture of the Boudhinath stupa in Kathmandu.

Mum and daughter on top of a pass on the way to Kailash.

I've been sick seven times now Mummy." Iona handed me the pathetic little clear plastic bag of regurgitated water, and I emptied it out of the Landcruiser window onto the Tibetan plateau. For the millionth time I wondered what I was doing here, several miles high and a harsh day's ride from the nearest hospital, with a six-year-old.

Iona was suffering from altitude sickness. I had been warned in Kathmandu of the serious dangers by Dr Buddha Basnyat, the world's leading authority on the subject. "You realise the worst-case scenario is high altitude pulmonary oedema or cerebral oedema [HAPE or HACE] which can result in death, don't you?" he warned me.

Yes, I realised. But I had brought her nonetheless. Why?

Before departure, I had made a list of the pros and cons of taking Iona to Tibet. The list of pros was very long. The cons had one main deadweight entry: sickness.

Well, I reasoned, of course she would get sick. Children get sick wherever they are. And we were not entering the complete unknown. Before having children I had travelled and walked throughout Tibet. It's all very well giving children domestic security, I reasoned – but what about teaching them something about the big, wide world, too? Iona had enjoyed India, China and Tibet when she was a baby and toddler, so I was already

**WIND HORSES**
These are flimsy pieces of rice paper (about 2 inches square) with horses stamped on them. They denote good luck and are thrown in the air in auspicious places – usually when walking along the tops of passes.

experienced in hacking through guilt trips and panic attacks when she was sick in strange places. I consulted my intuition: it told me Iona would be sick, but not dangerously so, and she would recover rapidly.

"As a general rule, if parents have been to a place before and know what they are letting themselves in for, then it's OK to take kids there. You know how to deal with the fact that it's filthy, there are no seat-belts on the buses and so on," says Glenn Rowley of KE Adventure Travel. He has led parties of sixth-formers to the top of Stok Kangri and taken his own children – the youngest aged six – up Langtang Valley in Nepal: places he knows like the back of his hand.

We were on higher ground, but not necessarily morally so. "I personally wouldn't take mine up that high," commented Glenn. Now we were cutting up through the Himalayas, traversing four of the world's highest passes in one day. The lack of oxygen in the thin air was making Iona woozy. She had a headache and was fatigued.

As HAPE occurs when the kidneys malfunction, the most important thing was to keep them working by making sure she kept on drinking purified water from the aerial of her telephone-shaped water vessel – and peeing.

At the top of the highest pass, the solid silence in the vehicle was punctuated only by Iona's sobbing. I held her like a baby, offering her water. Normally at the top of passes we'd shout: "Lha-so-so-so!" – 'May the gods be victorious!' – and throw wind horses. Now we all – including our Tibetan driver – breathed a collective sigh of relief as we charged past the macramé of bright prayer flags and began the only real cure for altitude sickness there is – descent.

By the time we had descended just a few hundred metres, Iona was visibly regenerating, and though she was still a bit wobbly, she slept well that night and was throwing snowballs at our fellow travellers the following morning. Phew: my intuition had been correct. "You were right," Lyn Fisk, who has been a health visitor in south Wales for 30 years, reassured me. "We've lost our intuition about when a child is ill or not. To allow the immune system to work, you have to allow the body to find its own level. If there's still a problem after 48 hours, you need help. But mostly children pull through within 24 hours."

"What if she gets sick?" was the question most commonly asked by friends and family before we left the UK. We prepared as well as we could: we had all the injections and sugar cubes required. Measles and other common illnesses regarded as harmless in the UK can be killers in the east. Dr Dan Rainbow, a Brighton GP who recently visited Tibet, and who is planning to take his 16-month-old daughter to Asia next year, advises: "Be realistic and flexible about travel plans. This obviously depends on a number of factors, including your child's age, whether they have any medical conditions, your previous experiences and the degree to which you are prepared to take risks. All foreign travel involves an element of risk, but a balance can be found between these and the experiences you gain by taking them – after all, isn't that what travelling is all about? These can only be personal decisions."

As it turned out, I'd exposed Iona to a little more risk than I had realised. It had been a scary passage, and one which I would not care to repeat. But for now, we were in Tibet, and prepared to enjoy ourselves. The fact that I was taking her out of class was a bit of a mystery to the other mothers at the school gates, but Iona took everything, from the stinky toilets to the funny food, in her stride.

# Fact file

## MEDICAL KIT

Health is of course the primary concern with children. But rather than make it an excuse not to go, why not see it as a surmountable challenge? When I took Iona to India as a baby, the medical kit took up more space than my clothes – but I used everything except the antibiotics and the medical insurance.
Here's a list of what I always pack...
● A good, comprehensive insurance policy
● Antibiotics: consult your doctor before you go. Most common are a broad-spectrum antibiotic for any infection and Flagyl for severe gut problems
● Water-sterilising tablets/drops
● Thermometer: a strip one travels well, but bear in mind they're not so accurate
● Calpol
● Sterile bandage
● Electrolyte solution (rehydration)
● Support bandage
● Chamomile – tea for nausea, drops for teething
● Calendula and lavender cream for cuts and rashes
● Cling film
● Tea tree oil for everything from fungal to viral infections – dilute three or four drops in a litre of sterilised water
● Homeopathic remedies, eg arsen alb for bumps and bruises
● Bach flower remedies – even if you don't believe in them, the placebo factor is high! Rescue remedy for everything, walnut for change, rock rose for nightmares etc
● Mint tea for stomach upsets
● Be prepared to buy local garlic and honey (natural antibiotics) and ginger (tea for upset tummy) for home remedies
● Antibacterial wipes: but the packaging can be bulky, so why not carry a lavender/TCP-soaked flannel around to wipe their hands with from time to time, and sterilise it every night?
● Your own needles for ultra-emergencies in third world countries

## SUN PROTECTION
● Hat
● Long-sleeved and trousers
● Sunscreen – factor 25 is enough (50 can block pores and cause nasty rashes). Re-apply every two hours.
● Sunshade for push-chair/baby backpack
● Calamine lotion for sunburn – though if you're in a place where aloe vera grows, use it!

● UV swimsuit
Stay in the shade during the hottest part of the day.

## JABS AND MOZZIES
Once children are weaned, injections are worth serious consideration. See your practice nurse about what you will require, but bear in mind that she/he will be looking at a chart which lists *all* the diseases a country harbours, regardless of the region, time of year etc. The most common inoculations will be:
● Polio   ● Tetanus
● Typhoid   ● Hepatitis A
● Diphtheria   ● BCG (for TB)
● Hepatitis B
● Meningococcal A & C – a one-off injection which lasts three years
● Japanese encephalitis (found in pig-rearing and rice-growing areas)
● Polio – found in poor areas
● Rabies – this involves three doses in a month (days 1, 14, 28).
● Malaria tablets
Malaria is likely in a low-lying swampy area in the summer months but is completely impossible in a high area in the winter. Malaria tablets almost invariably have some nasty side effects but mosquito bites abroad are inevitably worse than the home-grown variety. Nonetheless, you can repel mosquitoes by cutting sugar out of your children's diet, either taking a pot of Marmite with you or taking vitamin B tablets, using citronella oil, long-sleeved shirts and mosquito nets at dawn and dusk (when mozzies are most active).

## PACKING IT ALL IN
Think weight, space and versatility: a natty little roll-up changing mat is, after all, only an upbeat plastic bag. If you are going to be in any way adventurous, consider the following:
● Travel kettle/lightweight stove, pot and mugs
● Favourite toys – let them pack a small bag
● Favourite pillowcase, either for an inflatable pillow or can be stuffed with their clothes for the next day
● Familiar plates and cutlery for the children
● Familiar foods which require only the addition of milk or water, eg pasta and cereals
● A personal torch for each child

## WATER
Be very careful what you drink. Mineral water is now available everywhere, but their plastic bottles litter every Indian railway embankment and mountains of them lurk at the back of every Thai beach. The commercialisation of Himalayan springs means that many village women have to walk miles for the family water. Consider the implications. If you take your own container, you can regularly fill up with boiled, filtered or sterilised water. If you are travelling in a vehicle, use a container with a pipe/straw attachment to avoid wet clothes, and when walking you can carry your water in specially-designed 'holster'.

## ALTITUDE SICKNESS
You can find information on altitude sickness from Dr. Buddha Basnyat's clinic website at www.nepalinternationalclinic.com

## NAPPIES
You can buy disposables from India to Mexico, but they might end up choking a cow or ruining a beautiful Pacific beach. I travelled for six months with Terries and a bucket, which took up less space than three months' supply of Pampers. Terries dry and bleach beautifully in the Asian sun and were much easier on the conscience. If you can't face washing them out yourself, you can provide employment for someone at a very small cost.

## WINGING IT
Air fares for children under two are 10 per cent of full fare, but they won't have a seat for this – a seatbelt attached to yours, plus a 'basinet' carry-cot which is fixed somewhat precariously to the cabin wall in front of you. Fares rise to 67 per cent on their second birthday but they do get a seat and full luggage allowance. The advantages of travelling with children is that you (usually) get to board first and flight attendants are (usually) very helpful.
If you're long-hauling it, take activities to amuse them on the plane and allow them to wander round as much as they like between meals. If you have a stop-over, make sure you have snacks, drinks and something for a makeshift bed – a small shawl, blanket, for example. During take-off and landing the air pressure on the ears can be painful. The only way to alleviate this is to keep their jaws moving – chewing gum works with older children, and breast/bottle-feeding is best for babies. In-betweeners do well on sweets.

Above: Mount Kailash from the south.  Below: pausing for breath at the top of Dolma La pass following a 5-hour climb.

Dr Sheryle Bergmann Drewe, associate professor at the University of Manitoba, Canada, has taken her young daughter Kate all over the world. She has a doctorate in education, and is keen to stress the distinction between education and schooling. "The educational value of a trip to an exotic place wins hands down over the traditional schooling experience," she claims. "The experience of different cultures simply cannot be replicated in a school environment. You understand the purpose of learning another language when you have to speak it. Geography, history, mathematics, religion, day-to-day life – you can read in a text, or you can live it. Which one is going to make a difference?"

We arrived in Lhasa with several days'-worth of filthy washing. Iona loved helping me pump the water out, though it was too cold for her to stamp on it with her bare feet for more than a couple of minutes. While I hung out the washing Iona occupied herself by chasing Jigme, who worked in the hotel office, round the courtyard with a balloon full of water. While I took a shower, they drank chang (weak barley beer) together. "You've got such a big nose, all the snow will sit on it when you go to Mount Kailash!" he told her. "And you're a squash-nose!" returned Iona with delight. Though politically incorrect, they were great friends.

Soon Iona learnt enough Tibetan to bargain competently with the Tibetans – and always got the price she named. Looking for her in the main temple, I found her being lifted up by two grinning monks in order to flash her camera right in the sacred face of Tibet's holiest statue. I wouldn't dare take photographs in there, but Iona's little walking boots scrabbled confidently on the altar and the statue merely smiled indulgently.

The veteran traveller Dervla Murphy took her daughter through Pakistan on horseback when she was six, and remarks, in her book *Where the Indus is Young*: '...the five- to seven-year-old stage is ideal for travelling rough with small children. Under-fives are not physically mature enough for exposure to the unavoidable health hazards, while over-sevens tend to be much less philosophical in

## "Iona walked around Mount Kailash – 36 miles in four days, at a base altitude higher than any mountain in the Alps..."

Iona and friend outside the Jokhang temple.

their reactions to the inconveniences and strange customs of far-flungery.'

Six-year-olds can also walk surprising distances. In the 'far-flungery' of western Tibet, Iona walked around Mount Kailash – 36 miles in four days, at a base altitude higher than any mountain in the Alps. True, I had to carry her for five hours up the longest and steepest pass, but she just sat there sipping oxygen, and would not hear of turning back. Strangely, it's the simple things, like getting on and off buses, which cause the worst nightmares. At Delhi airport, our bus arrived like a thunderbolt from the blue, scattered the assembled Indians and screeched to a halt inches from where Iona slept on our trolley. It reminded me of a moment in Ms Murphy's book when her daughter's horse Hallam rears up over a precipice, the young Indus boiling several thousand feet below. You could say it's not fair to expose children to such dangers, but it's also true that we take risks every day, and because they come

in familiar guises: orange lollies, kids' programmes, driving cars, social breakdown – we don't recognise them as such.

Any modern parent with even one tincy-wincy baby knows what it's like to survey the slag heap of paraphernalia, worthy of a Himalayan expedition, without which it is impossible to stay with relatives for the weekend. Quite honestly, you might as well go the whole hog and actually go to the Himalayas. Or, if you haven't faced the flies, the filth and the poverty before, perhaps a short jaunt to France, Greece or the Rockies? If you can look after a child at home it's actually easier when travelling. For one thing, as the usual pulls on your time are absent, you get to spend more time together. If your child is upset by something, you have time to explain; if your child makes a joke, you have time to laugh – even in the middle of the night. As Dr Rainbow says: "Travelling with a child is just like all parenting – a matter of common sense." Yes – and with just a hint of the unknown, too.